H E R AISED M E U P

TO STAND
— ON —
MOUNTAINS

HELEN GRACE
LESCHEID

Helen Grace Lescheid

PUBLISHING

Belleville, Ontario, Canada

TO STAND ON MOUNTAINS
Copyright © 2005, Helen Grace Lescheid

All Scripture quotations, unless otherwise specified, are from the HOLY BIBLE, NEW INTERNATIONAL VERSION ®. Copyright © 1973, 1978, 1984 by International Bible Society. Used by permission of Zondervan Publishing House. All rights reserved. • Scripture quotations marked AMP are taken from *The Amplified Bible*, Old Testament, copyright © 1965, 1987 by the Zondervan Corporation. *The Amplified New Testament*, copyright © 1954, 1958, 1987 by the Lockman Foundation. Used by permission. • Scripture quotations marked NLT are taken from *Life Application Study Bible*, New Living Translation. Copyright © 1996. Used by permission of Tyndale House Publishers, Inc., Wheaton, IL 60187. All rights reserved. Scripture quotations marked ESV are taken from The *ESV Classic Reference Bible*. Copyright @ 2001 by Crossway Bibles, a division of Good News Publishers. All rights reserved.Scripture marked TM are taken from *The Message*, copyright © by Eugene H. Peterson, 1993, 1994, 1995. Used by permission of NavPress Publishing Group. Scripture quotations marked NRSV are from the *New Revised Standard Version* of the Bible, copyright 1989, by the Division of Christian Education of the National Council of the Churches of Christ in the United States of America, and are used by permission. All rights reserved. Scripture quotations marked NRSV are from the *New Revised Standard Version* of the Bible, copyright 1989, by the Division of Christian Education of the National Council of the Churches of Christ in the United States of America, and are used by permission. All rights reserved. Scripture quotations marked CEV are from the *Contemporary English Version*, copyright © 1995, by American Bible Society.

Library and Archives Canada Cataloguing in Publication

Lescheid, Helen Grace

    To stand on mountains / Helen Grace Lescheid.

Includes memoirs from the author, and others.
ISBN 1-55306-980-3

    1. Christian life. 2. Christian life--Biblical teaching.
I. Title.

BV4501.3.L48 2005   248.8'6   C2005-904157-9

For more information or
to order additional copies, please contact:
Helen Grace Lescheid
17-1973 Winfield Drive
Abbotsford, B.C., V3G 1K6
E-mail:lescheid @uniserve.com

Essence Publishing is a Christian Book Publisher dedicated to furthering the work of Christ through the written word. For more information, contact: 20 Hanna Court, Belleville, Ontario, Canada K8P 5J2. Phone: 1-800-238-6376. Fax: (613) 962-3055.
E-mail: publishing@essencegroup.com.
Internet: www.essencegroup.com

Contents

Forgiveness

Prayer

Acknowledgements

My heartfelt thanks to:

The many people who've shared their stories with me—stories of struggle and ultimately triumph. My life has been enriched and blessed by their candour.

Editors of many magazines (named in the references) who've worked with me on the stories. A special thanks to Lori Mackay of Essense Publishing, who has spent many hours helping me put together this book. I've learned so much from you all.

Teddy McCrea, whose expertise in photography provided the cover photo.

My many readers, whose encouraging comments are like a cup of cold water on a day of wilderness writing.

To God, without whose intervention there would be no writer and no stories to tell.

Preface

I waited patiently for the LORD;
he turned to me and heard my cry.
He lifted me out of the slimy pit,
out of the mud and mire;
he set my feet on a rock
and gave me a firm place to stand.
Psalm 40:1,2

I was standing in the Old Growth Forest near Nelson, British Columbia, staring at a most extraordinary pine tree. The base of the tree rested on a huge boulder like a giant sitting on a chair. The bark was split open like a brown cloak on either side of the rock. The tree, like a grinning champion after a noble fight, stood triumphantly on top of its enemy.

I laughed at the tree's audacity.

I imagined the fight. Many years ago, at the edge of a boulder, like a menacing mountain, a small seed sprouted in the ground. What chance did it have to grow up? Still, it pushed its way through the ground. As it grew in size it kept bumping into a rocky wall, a constant reminder of its unyielding, ornery neighbour. If it had been like us, it might have grumbled, "What did I do to deserve this? I can't even stretch and grow like other pine trees around me." But it kept growing and reaching and stretching and climbing, one inch at a time. Right on top of the boulder! Thus elevated, it continued to grow, perfectly straight, with the rest of the trees.

Now, the tree seemed to be saying to me, "If you can't move it or tunnel through it, use it to your advantage. Turn a stumbling stone into a stepping stone."

I was reminded of the story of Caleb, who exhibited this kind of daring faith. Along with eleven other scouts, he'd been sent to spy out the Promised Land for Moses.

When they returned, ten of the scouts who focussed on the boulders in their path brought back a negative report. "The people living there are powerful, and their cities and towns are fortified and very large," they said. "Giants live there, and we look like grasshoppers to them. If we attempt to enter the land, we'll most certainly perish."

But Caleb held up his hand to quiet the people. He shouted, "Don't be afraid of the people of the land. They are only helpless prey to us! They have no protection, but the LORD is with us! Don't be afraid of them!"[1] "Let us go up at once to occupy it, for we are well able to overcome it."[2] But the people could not be persuaded. Refusing to take the risk of daring faith, they died in the wilderness.

Notice, where Caleb got his confidence: "the LORD is with us." His boldness rested on his understanding of God, not on his own abilities. Never once did he lose sight of this, even during forty years of aimless wandering in the wilderness. When he finally did enter the Promised Land, he requested of Joshua not the easy valleys but the rough terrain where the giants lived. His firm belief was "the LORD helping me, I will drive them out just as he said."[3]

When others saw obstacles, Caleb saw opportunities. When the majority caved in to discouragement, Caleb's faith continued to burn brightly. When others chose the easy path, Caleb said, "Give me this mountain!"

In this book I share my own experiences and the experiences of others who've kindly shared their lives with me, people who've struggled and overcome life's distressing inequities, trials, and disappointments. At times they battle discouragement, loneliness, and fear. But in the midst of it all, they know one thing for sure: "the LORD is with us." Thus fortified, they've learned to ride the waves of life. Instead of blaming unfortunate circumstances, they've accepted them as part of God's plan for their lives. They've taken the risk of daring faith.

What is keeping you from becoming the person you want to be? Do you blame it on a mountain in your path? Circumstances that seem to block you at every turn?

In reading this book, may you find insights and assurance that you, too, can turn obstacles into opportunities. Take the risk of daring faith. Like the tree, find a way to stand upon your mountain. God wants to raise you up to more than you have been.

Special Challenges

I love you, O Lord, my strength.

The Lord is my rock, my fortress,
and my deliverer,
my God, my rock in whom I take refuge...

By you I can crush a troop,
and by my God I can leap over a wall.

This God—his way is perfect;
the promise of the Lord proves true;
he is a shield for all who take refuge in him.

PSALM 18:1,2,29,30 NRSV

Each new day is a new beginning—
to learn more about ourselves
to care more about others,
to laugh more than we did,
to accomplish more than we thought we could,
and to be more than we were before.

AUTHOR UNKNOWN

The Landlady's Christmas Gift[4]

Forging ahead through driving November rains, I hurried to my home in Vancouver, British Columbia. Home was a basement suite I rented in a large old house. When I flicked on the lights, I noticed something peculiar on my small kitchen table. A cooking pot had been turned upside down, revealing blistered handles. "Will you be more careful?" said a note. "Turn down the gas when food begins to boil." It was signed by Lily, the landlady.

Tears sprang to my eyes. All afternoon, I'd jostled crowds in noisy shopping malls, seeking a perfect Christmas gift for my mother, but every time I'd come upon something I knew she'd like, it was too expensive for me. Saving money for nursing school and living expenses didn't leave me much for Christmas gifts. Totally discouraged, I'd taken the bus home. It seemed unfriendly to me to ride shoulder to shoulder with people without saying a word, so I'd started a conversation with the woman beside me. She'd answered me curtly, then stared out the window as though wanting to be left alone. Then I came home to find this rebuke from my landlady.

A country girl living on her own in the big city of Vancouver—the idea seemed so glamorous a few months ago. Now, crushing loneliness overwhelmed me. I threw myself across my bed behind a curtain and sobbed my heart out.

Eventually, I lay there thinking and praying about a suitable gift for my mother. Suddenly I remembered a conversation I'd overheard at work. Some women had discussed a home party they'd attended. A saleswoman had come to demonstrate her wares and, because sales had reached a certain amount, the hostess received a lace tablecloth for her efforts. "There were only about ten people there," the woman had said, "but it's surprising how fast sales mount up when everybody buys a little."

A lace tablecloth! What could be more perfect for my mother for Christmas? I could just see her worn hands smooth it across the table in our old farmhouse kitchen. On Christmas day, as on other special occasions, she'd place roast chicken still hot in its juices on that table (we couldn't afford turkey), mashed potatoes whipped with an egg until they glistened, spicy crabapples, featherlight buns, German *pfeffernuesse* and *lebkuchen*...

The more I thought about that lace tablecloth, the more I wanted it. But a home party? Could I pull that off? I'd never done anything like that before. Besides, who would come to it?

Well, there were people at church. I didn't know anybody there really well, but they might come. And then there were the women I'd had lunch with at work. I counted them up: yes, there were at least ten.

"Oh, Lord, if this is Your will, give me the courage to do it," I prayed.

Still full of self-doubt, I booked a party. Encouraged by the saleswoman's enthusiastic response, I distributed my carefully written invitations at church and at work.

The day of the party in early December dawned heavy and grey. I decorated my scrubbed basement suite with cedar boughs and placed a red candle and Christmas napkins besides the dishes I'd borrowed from the landlady. By evening, my place smelled of cedar, chocolate brownies, and coffee.

Half an hour before the party was to start, the saleswoman arrived with a load of boxes. I helped her carry them inside, and soon a lovely display of colourful kitchenware and toys decorated my bed, the only flat area big enough.

I offered the woman a cup of coffee. Cradling my own mug in clammy hands, I glanced at the clock again with one ear cocked to outside noises. Where were my guests? Only five minutes to go, and nobody had come yet.

Promptly at 7:30, the door burst open; it was Lily, the landlady. Her eyes swept the empty room, and she blurted out, "Where is everybody?"

"I don't know, Lily," I stammered. "Nobody has come yet."

"Well, we can't wait much longer," she said and stomped out of the room.

I groaned inwardly, thinking that I should have known better than to book a party.

"I suppose we'll call it off," the saleswoman said as she rose and began to gather up her wares.

Apologizing for the inconvenience I'd caused her, I helped her pack. Toys swam before my eyes. Embarrassment burned my cheeks.

Suddenly, I heard a noise outside, and the door opened, framing two women I'd never seen before. "Hi. We live down the street. Lily tells us there's a party here."

Bewildered, I asked them to take a seat.

During the next ten minutes, this scenario repeated itself several times. The room filled with people. I stared incredulously at each unfamiliar yet friendly face. Finally, Lily herself returned, wearing a grin, and winked at me.

Over coffee, the buzzing of animated voices reminded me of other gatherings of friendly people at home in the country.

"Going home for Christmas?" somebody asked me.

When I shook my head no, Lily quickly intercepted: "I'd like you to have turkey dinner with us. And by the way, next week we're having a Christmas cantata at church. Are you interested?" Other invitations followed for coffee and Christmas baking.

I could hardly grasp the goodwill of these people who, an hour ago, had been total strangers to me. *Perhaps people seem unfriendly because they've lacked opportunity to prove otherwise,* I mused.

Oh, you're wondering about the lace tablecloth? When the sales were totalled, I had enough for the coveted hostess gift. For many years, my mother decked her old table with it, and her face revealed the pride and gratitude she felt.

But Lily herself gave the greatest gift that Christmas: underneath her brusque manner lay a warm, caring heart that reached out to ease my loneliness. Lily gave me a gift for my mother and a home at Christmas.

Celebrate the Light[5]

The Second World War raged in Europe during Christmas Eve in 1944.

Mother, with four small children, had fled our native Ukraine with the retreating German army. Father had been reported missing in action.

Now we were refugees living in a two-room shack in Dieterwald, Poland. But again the fighting front was only about fifty kilometres away. Frequent air raids sent us scurrying for cover. Explosions rattled the windows. Army trucks brought in the wounded and the dead. Hay wagons filled with refugees rumbled west; bombers droned overhead and army tanks rolled east. Partisans (underground resistance) attacked innocent women and children at night.

Nobody in his right mind went out into the dark winter night.

And yet, it was Christmas Eve. Two women had prepared a Christmas party in a neighbouring village and invited us. Mother, wanting to give us children joy, accepted.

She instructed my sister and me to dress warmly against the winter's cold. "Tonight we're going to a party," she said. Being only eight years old, I sensed no danger—only wondrous excitement.

Hurriedly, my sister, two years younger, and I dressed. If only Mother would hurry! A simple wick flickered in a saucer of oil—our only light. We could barely see her shadowy form as she bustled about getting my four-year-old brother, Fred, and almost two-year-old sister, Katie, ready.

Finally, Mother was putting on her heavy winter coat, kerchief, and warm felt boots.

With one small breath, she blew out the oil lamp. It was pitch dark now.

"Open the door, Lena," she called to me.

We stepped onto the crisp snow covering the farmyard. A moon crescent hung above a large house across the yard where the estate owners lived—kind people who treated us refugees well. It, too, was shrouded in darkness.

Mother lifted Katie and shuffled her to her back; she'd carry her piggyback for the five kilometres.

"Hang tight onto my coat collar," she coaxed. Then, turning towards us girls, she said, "You take Fred's hands." My younger sister and I complied. We had often taken care of our little brother while Mother had culled potatoes in the big barns or had done other chores for the landowners.

At the road, we stopped. Although I knew it well from my treks to school, I could barely make out the houses on either side of the street. No street lights were allowed now. Windows heavily draped permitted no light to seep out of the houses.

My mother hesitated for a brief moment. Then she said, "Come, we'll take the shortcut across the fields."

The snow crunched as four pairs of feet punched holes in the white expanse of open fields. Stars spangled the vault of sky above us. A blood-red glow smeared the eastern sky. At times, an explosion sent flames shooting into the sky.

"Girls, recite your poems to me." Mother's voice sounded a bit shaky. Her arms aching, she put Katie down on the snowy ground. Our recitations of Christmas poems made white puffs in the cold night air.

When we finished, Mother said, "Speak up loud and clear when your turn comes. No mumbling."

She lifted Katie once more onto her back, and we began to walk again. On and on we walked. But we were far too excited to be tired.

Finally, we arrived at our friends' house. The door opened, and we stepped inside. I felt I had stepped into heaven itself. Lights! A whole roomful of lights. Candlelight flickered from a small Christmas tree and bounced out of happy children's eyes. Heavily-draped windows kept the light inside—for us to revel in. Red paper chains decked the tree; delicate paper cherubs smiled down upon us.

We squeezed in amongst children and women sitting on the floor.

Soon the room filled with singing: "*Stille Nacht, Heilige Nacht*" (Silent Night, Holy Night). "*Welch ein Jubel, welche Freude...*" Some mothers sang alto, the rest of us, soprano. We sang, with gusto and from memory, songs that lifted our hearts above the terrors of war and inspired new hope for the days ahead.

I can't remember our long trek home that night, but I do remember the wonderful gifts I received. My right pocket bulged with the most beautiful ball I'd ever seen. A very colourful ball it was. Much later, I learned it had been made out of scrunched-up rags wrapped in rainbow-coloured yarn, probably gleaned from unravelling old sweaters. The other pocket held three cookies!

Soon after that wonderful Christmas party, we were evacuated. Icy winds blew snow into our faces as we cowered on an uncovered hay wagon pulled by two scrawny horses. With the front so close behind, we travelled day and night. Once it was safe to stop, we slept in drafty barns. We ate hunks of frozen bread and drank the occasional cup of milk supplied by a Red Cross jeep.

But the warm memory of that Christmas celebration shone like a small candle in the darkness.

Even years later, when my own life's circumstances seemed too bleak to celebrate Christmas, I remembered the truth of Christmas born in my heart that night: Jesus, the light of the world, came to us at Christmastime, and no amount of darkness can put out that light.

Why Be Afraid?[6]

My eighty-seven-year-old great-aunt, Anna, has lived a contented life despite great hardships and dangers. As a refugee fleeing for her life during the Second World War, she barely escaped with her life. As a pioneer in the Paraguayan jungle, she slept peacefully despite the dangers lurking in the night just outside her makeshift shelter. As a new immigrant in Canada, she was not afraid to walk to church in the dark or to stay home alone. "Why aren't you afraid?" I asked her one day.

"Oh, I used to be afraid—of many things," she smiled. "That was before I experienced..." she paused, her eyes taking on a peculiar lustre. "But it was so many years ago," she shrugged, as though wanting to change the subject. My curiosity piqued, I encouraged Aunt Anna to continue. We settled back into the sofa cushions, and she began to tell me the following story.

Three weeks before Christmas 1944—the memory is as vivid today as though it happened yesterday—I was a refugee from the Ukraine, living in an old house high up in the Alps near Ratkersburg, Yugoslavia.

The Second World War had unleashed its fury upon my village of Nieder-Chortitza, west of the Dnieper River in the Ukraine. After many months of bombing and shelling, we had fled for our lives. In the dim interior of a freight car, we tried to calm our pounding hearts by singing hymns. Our train, crammed with refugees, had inched its way across the Ukrainian steppes and through Poland. Sometimes the Russian army opened fire on the train. Bombs exploded and rocked the cars. The staccato of machine guns drummed in our heads. We clung to each other.

But we had made it safely to Yugoslavia, now occupied by the Germans. Since the Germans had brought us and treated us favourably, the Yugoslavs hated us. We feared partisan activity against us—an underground anti-German movement. Wild stories circulated about how these men, dressed as firemen, had raped refugee women and plundered their homes at night. Some of our boys had been shot at by them. For that reason we kept our doors bolted shut. Women never travelled alone.

Added to this peril, the fighting front was again too close for comfort. Many nights, searchlights fanned the night skies, then explosions rocked the windows as the Russian bombers dropped their deadly cargo.

Once more, we feared for our lives and thought about evacuation.

"Come to Germany," my sister Tina had written. "You'll be safer here."

So, on this particular day, a friend and I took a train to Graz, Austria, to fill out application forms for a visa. The long, dangerous journey took all day. On the return trip to Ratkersburg, I noticed how quickly daylight was fading. Then sleet pelted the window.

"A miserable night to be out walking," my friend muttered.

I agreed.

"I'm getting off at the next station to spend the night at my son's house," she said. "Anna, you're welcome to come too."

I shook my head no. My friends at home would worry if I didn't arrive tonight, and I had no way of telling them about a change in plans.

The train slowed, and my friend got off. Watching her receding back as she hurried away, I felt desolate. Should I have gone with her? The train lurched and began to move again. At eight p.m., it chugged into my station. As I descended, an icy wind tore at my threadbare coat and thin kerchief. The sleet stung my face. I hurried into the dimly lit station, sat down on a wooden bench, and deliberated what to do.

To get back to my home up the mountain, I would have to walk ten kilometres, alone, in the pitch darkness. I had no flashlight, and I would have to find my way. Even worse, the narrow path ran past a cemetery, vineyards, and dense forest—the kinds of places partisans might be hiding in. Only a few houses lay scattered on the lonely terrain. Then, too, I would have to ford a rushing mountain stream.

There's no way I can make that trip tonight, I thought.

A middle-aged man busied himself behind the wicket. Timidly, I approached him: "Sir, could I spend the night here, please?"

"No, ma'am," he said emphatically.

"I have far to walk..." I began.

"Ma'am, I can't allow it," he said abruptly. He grabbed his coat and hat and fished for the keys in his pocket. Then he headed for the door. Panic kept me rooted to the floor. *I can't go up that mountain alone.*

At the door the man turned and said impatiently, "C'mon. I'm locking this place up." He must have seen the panic in my eyes, for he said more kindly, "During an air raid, you'll be safer up the mountain anyway."

As I listened to the receding crunch of his boots on gravel, the knot of fear in my stomach tightened. The only man who could have helped me vanished into the night.

What was I to do? For a few moments, I stood under the eaves of the straw roof. Then I lifted my face to the sky and spoke to the only Person who could help me now. "Father," I whispered, "I'm so scared. Take away this terror. Walk with me."

Suddenly a light fanned across the sky.

Oh, no, the bombers! I thought. Knowing that train stations are targeted, I moved away from the building.

The light moved with me, clearly shining on my path.

I waited for the screeching of planes, then the explosion of bombs. Nothing. Instead, a deep quietness. An indescribable peace filled my heart, dispelling every trace of fear. The path lay bright at my feet.

Hymns of praise welled up inside me: "*Lass die Herzen immer froehlich und mit Dank erfuellet sein*" (May our hearts be ever joyful and filled with thankfulness); "*So nimm denn meine Haende und fuehre mich*" (Take Thou my hand, O Father, and lead me on). Song after joyous song filled me with praise. I fought a strong urge to sing out loud—after all, one had to be prudent—but I began to hum softly.

Then I realized the wind had stopped—and the rain. In fact, it was as warm as a summer's night. I began to loosen my kerchief. *How strange to be so warm in December*, I thought.

When I reached the swollen stream, the water glistened like a myriad of diamonds. Sure-footed, I stepped onto the flat rocks sticking out of the foaming water and forded it.

The light guided and cheered me all the way up the mountain. As I neared the old house, I looked back over the treacherous mountain path I had taken. Like a ribbon of light, it lay behind me.

Excitedly, I knocked on the door. I wanted my friends to see this awesome sight.

The door opened. A gust of wind grabbed it, almost tearing it off its hinges. "Anna, come in," my friend yelled, pulling me inside.

My friends crowded around me. "Such a terrible storm. Weren't you afraid?" they asked.

"No," I shook my head. "There was no storm."

But I could say no more, for now I could hear it too: the howling wind, the sleet pelting the window panes, the moaning of the house.

While one friend busied herself with my supper, another took my coat. "It's dry," she said. "Anna, your coat is dry."

"I know," I said. I did my best to explain, but my friends looked at me strangely as though they were trying to make sense out of it all."

My aunt suddenly became very shy. "You do believe this really happened to me?"

"Yes, I believe you." I squeezed her hand. "Your story

reminds me of the Bible verse, "The angel of the Lord encamps around those who fear him, and he delivers them."[7]

"Yes, yes, that's true," Aunt Anna smiled. "Then what is there to be afraid of?"

Never Alone

It was May 8, 1945, the day the Second World War ended.

A mass exodus of refugees, anxious to leave a communist country, plugged the village streets near Celje, Yugoslavia. German soldiers, eager to go home to their loved ones, laid down their weapons and walked toward the border between Yugoslavia and Austria. My mother, Neta Dyck, sister, Tina Vogt, her small son Viktor, and I joined the crowds trying to make their way into Austria.

Men, women and children, carrying all their worldly possessions in burlap bags, pushed past others pulling small wagons. Army trucks and jeeps, overflowing with German soldiers and civilians, were inching through the crowds. It was bedlam. I hurried to keep up with my family. During the eighteen months of our fleeing from Ukraine, we'd managed to stay together. I feared being separated now.

The sun was shining; still, there was a cool breeze. I buttoned the light maroon coat I was wearing over a blue cotton dress. I wore a light pair of sandals and carried a burlap sack that contained a blanket and a pillow. I carried no food, for we expected to be in another refugee camp in Klagenfurt, Austria, by nightfall. Viktor, my seven-year-old nephew, took my hand. "Tante Annie, I'm so tired," he whispered. I picked him up. His thin arms circled my neck and his cheek rested on my shoulder.

A blaring of horns made me move aside. An army truck was trying to pass. My mother, white hair spilling out of a kerchief, stepped forward, "Please, sir, take us along," she begged. "The child is tired."

"Get on," the driver barked, "if you can find room."

I squeezed my body beside a soldier sitting on the floor, feeling suddenly shy when I almost landed in his lap. By the grin on his face, I could tell he didn't mind sharing space with a nineteen-year-old woman. The truck inched forward. Finally we arrived at the border.

Partisan soldiers, sympathetic with the communists, controlled the Yugoslav/Austrian border. "Stop!" one shouted, pointing his machine gun into the crowd. People froze. Trucks came to a halt. "Everybody out," he ordered. Partisans searched everyone. Old women and small children were allowed back on the trucks. Young people, like myself, were ordered to walk—but not across the border—back to the village where we'd come from. I was stunned. So close to Austria and freedom, yet we were denied entrance. Worse still, I would be separated from my loved ones.

I picked up my sack and mustered a smile. "See you in the evening," I shouted to my mother, sister, and nephew on the truck. In the crowd I recognized two girls from my hometown, Maria and Helen Klassen. "Let's stay together," I whispered.

We marched for hours with partisans on horseback moving beside us and shouting, "Keep pace." Darkness fell. On a football field outside of a village, we hunkered down for the night. I wrapped myself in my blanket and tried to sleep, but I couldn't stop shivering from the cold and fright. What were they going to do with us?

Day after day we marched. An old man collapsed on the road. I watched with horror as a guard pointed his gun at him and fired, then kicked his writhing body into the ditch.

Try as she might, Maria couldn't keep up. A guard jammed his rifle butt into her belly. She fell to the ground. He kicked her, then rode off. One German soldier helped her up and whispered, "Girls, get into the middle." From then on a small brigade of seven defeated German soldiers formed a shield around us and protected us. Moreover, they took care of us. When a strap on my flimsy sandals broke, a soldier handed me a pair of army boots. "Here, wear these," he said.

Day after day, the relentless march went on. We had no idea where we were going. We had no food or water. When we came to a stream, we scooped up handfuls of water and lapped it up. We pulled up weeds along the road and chewed on them. One of the soldiers, a medic, filled his canteen with water and added a little sugar. Then he gave it to us girls to drink. How much longer could we survive?

After eight days of marching, a man shouted, "Convoy, to the right." We moved aside to let a guard on horseback pass.

He pulled in the reins and stopped his horse. "Damn Germans," he shouted, pointed his gun into the crowd, and fired in my direction. A searing pain shot through me. Blood gushed from my legs. I crumpled to the ground.

I knew I was hurt, but I didn't find out how badly until later. (My left ankle was crushed, and embedded in my right leg were five pieces of shrapnel.) Dimly I heard a man's voice say, "Annie, open your mouth." I swallowed some pills and sugar water. Then the medic wrapped tourniquets around my legs and bandaged them.

I lost consciousness. Dimly I felt somebody slapping my face. A voice from faraway sounded. "Annie, I have to leave you," the medic said urgently. "The partisans will shoot me if I stay with you." I listened to the receding sound of feet pounding the gravel road. Then all was quiet.

Panic overwhelmed me, and I began to cry.

"Jesus, help me," I sobbed. I was alone, wounded, lying beside a road in a hostile country. Would the partisans shoot me and discard my body like they'd done with the old man?

Suddenly, I felt a warm Presence, like a mother hovering over a sick child. *"Don't be afraid; I am here,"* a Voice said. *"I will never leave you nor forsake you."*

"Then I am safe," I said softly. "With Jesus beside me, all will be well." An indescribable peace enveloped me.

Toward evening, a rumble of wheels made me raise my head. I saw an older man and his son jump off an oxen cart and approach me. "My God! She's been shot," the older man said. They lifted me up and placed me onto the cart, then drove to a hospital.

"We don't treat Germans here," an officer at the door said. "Take her to the partisan headquarters." There they were more interested in what I knew than in my wounds. I was interrogated for quite some time. When I answered in Russian, the interrogator looked surprised.

"How come you speak our language?"

"I was born in the Ukraine and learned Russian in school."

"So you ran away," he said. "You figured Germany would win this war."

"Yes," I said.

"Foolish girl," he sneered. "You could be at home in Russia eating white bread, and look at you now." His lips curled into a smirk. "You think only the Germans are good, right?"

"No, we had Russian neighbors back home, and they were good people," I said. "There are good people and bad people in every race."

He was silent for a long moment. "You're right," he said. He picked up a pen and began writing on a paper. Then he handed it to me. "You may go to the hospital now," he said. "A prisoner-of-war camp is no place for you."

The hospital had no X-ray machines. No equipment. A doctor (a German prisoner of war) put a cast on my left leg to above my knee, leaving a hole over the shattered ankle so my wound could be cleansed and dressed. They bandaged my right leg riddled with shrapnel. In this large open ward, every bed was full. Catholic sisters in black habits moved about bringing food and water to the patients. During visiting hours, civilians came to visit, but nobody came to see me. As I watched patients talking with their families, a great longing for my own family overwhelmed me. What had happened to my loved ones? Would I ever see them again?

A month later, my cast was removed, and a few days later, even though my wounds were still infected, I was discharged from hospital and sent to a refugee camp near Maribur. It was a big school gym, where we slept on the floor. Without crutches, I couldn't walk, but in the mornings two young girls put their hands together to form a little chair and carried me outside and placed me on the grass, and in the evening they returned to carry me back into the building. At noon an old man brought me a bowl of soup.

Day after day, the same senseless existence. People with hunched shoulders and sad faces shuffled by. Few bothered to talk to me, and I couldn't really blame them. By now the putrid bandages that stuck to my wounds smelled terrible. My left leg resembled the size of a stove pipe. Wild flesh grew from the wound in my right leg.

Feeling utterly helpless and forsaken, my life became unbearable. I wanted to die.

One day when the old man brought me my soup, I shook my head. "I'm not eating," I said. He dumped the soup onto the ground and stomped off. In a short while he returned with a doctor.

When he looked at my leg, he exclaimed, "Oh, my God! We've got to do something."

By bicycle Dr. Petrovich transported me to a hospital, where I was given a warm bath. My bandages were removed, and the doctor examined my wounds. "We may have to amputate your left leg," he said. But the next day when the doctor operated, he removed much pus and dead tissue, but my leg was spared.

Some weeks later, when the infection had cleared and my wounds had healed, I was discharged to the refugee camp where Dr. Petrovich was the doctor in residence. He requested that I work for him in the sick bay, and I was more than happy to do so. I made rounds with him, took temperatures, made up charts, gave out food and medications, held sick children, and did whatever jobs I could, even darning the doctor's socks and turning over his frayed shirt collar.

Watching me hobble down the hall, the doctor said, "Annie, walk on your toes, or you will always be limping." The pain was excruciating, but I forced myself to walk on tiptoes. I'll be forever grateful to Dr. Petrovich, for today I do not walk with a limp.

Moreover, this good doctor prevented my forceful return to Russia. When a Russian official came to take me away, he intercepted. "Annie is far too ill to be moved today," he said. The following day, he hurriedly formulated a plan of escape.

"I know a man who smuggles people across the border into Austria," he said. "You've been a great help to me, and I will do all I can to help you now." I'm not sure how he managed it, but Dr. Petrovich supplied the necessary papers and money, and I was ready to leave.

Just as I was leaving the sick bay, Herman—a man I'd worked with—brought me a letter. "My family doesn't know I'm still alive," he said. "Would you deliver this letter to my parents? They live near Graz, Austria." Of course! It was comforting to know I had a contact address to go to.

On the train I met another girl who was also going to Austria to search for her family. We decided to travel together. Miraculously, the border guards allowed us to cross without incident.

We stepped off the train into Austria and freedom!

But there was nobody waiting for us. An icy winter wind stung our faces and chilled us to the bone. We found shelter in a broken boxcar beside the train track. The following day, my friend prepared to walk to a refugee camp in hopes of finding her family. "Come with me," she said. "Maybe you will find your mother and sister there."

But I shook my head no. I had a letter to deliver.

Herman's parents were overjoyed to receive a letter from their son. They invited me to eat with them and stay the night. As I snuggled under the warm comforter, I thought, *Maybe they'll hire me.* They had a large house and a big farm and would surely welcome help with the chores. But the next morning when I offered my services, Herman's mother said, "We don't need a maid."

It was clear she wanted me to leave. But where to? "Go to the neighbour's," she shrugged. "They may need farm help."

Off I trudged over fields covered in snow to a farmhouse four kilometres away. It was bitterly cold, and my flimsy coat couldn't keep out the wind. Tears blinded my eyes and froze on my eyelashes. I was turned out by a woman for whom I'd gone out of my way to show a kindness. Such heartlessness was incomprehensible. Yes, I looked like a tramp with my shabby maroon coat and army boots, but I was willing to work hard for room and board. What if nobody hired me? Where would I go? "God, I have nobody but You," I prayed. "Please, help me find favour with some farmer."

At the next farmhouse, a heavy-set woman opened the door a crack. When I told her why I had come, she invited me inside the foyer. "Wait here while I talk with my husband," she said. On a wall hung a crucifix. As I stared at Jesus on the cross, tears welled up in my eyes. Yes, Jesus was here too; He would help me.

A small girl about six and her younger brother kept peering at me from behind a door. "Mama, the lady looks so sad," I heard the little girl say. "Please, let her stay."

And so, because of the kindness of a little girl, I was hired. I worked very hard cleaning out pig barns, washing laundry on a scrub board, cleaning the house, taking care of the children, and, in the spring, helping the farmer on the field.

But as time went on, I became restless to find my family. I had written letters to the Red Cross and to a hotel where one of my girlfriends had worked during the war. But nothing came of it. In the aftermath of war, postal delivery was sporadic. How would I ever find my family?

One evening the farmer's wife called out, "Annie, there's somebody at the door for you." Me? Who could be calling?

I peered into the darkness trying to identify a man and a woman standing at the door. "Annie, don't you recognize us?" the woman asked.

My eyes focused and I saw them: Suzie and Peter, from Nieder Chortitza, our village in the Ukraine! They had heard about me through the hotel to which I had written. Now they had come to ask me about their missing relatives. Well, I had no news for them, but they had wonderful news for me: they knew where my mother, my sister, and my nephew were—in a refugee camp in Treffling, not far away.

On a beautiful day in May, I stepped into the warm embrace of my mother. "Thank God, you're safe," she cried. "I was so worried, you being all alone—"

I smiled at her. In the days to come I would tell her how I'd really never been alone.

Annie Dyck

Editor's note: After Annie rejoined her family, she and her mother immigrated to British Columbia, Canada, where they bought a little house in Clearbrook and entertained many friends. Annie's mother died in 1982 in her ninety-fourth year. Annie still lives with her husband in Abbotsford, B.C. Sister Tina remained in Germany, where Viktor also lives with his family. You may be interested in knowing that Annie is the niece of Anna in "Why Be Afraid?"

Gems of Truth: Pass It On[8]

"He who refreshes others will himself be refreshed."[9]

A blizzard scooped up snow from the Ukrainian steppes and hurled it against the windowpanes of my childhood home. Inside our small kitchen, however, Mother had prepared a happy Easter surprise. An awestruck six-year-old, I gazed at the red, blue, green, and yellow Easter eggs nestled among a forest of rye shoots, five inches high, growing in a rusty old dishpan.

Not until I was an adult did I grasp the significance of my mother's creativity. During the early 1940s, I was too young to be worried about privations the Second World War had brought into our lives. Food was scarce; fuel was almost gone. Such luxuries as egg colouring could not be found. Mother had used onion skins, moss, a bleeding piece of fabric, and a few drops of ink. Despite our hardships, she had created a joyous Easter celebration for us children.

Two years later, my mother and all four children fled from our home in the Ukraine and eventually settled in Canada. Life became easier, and we no longer worried about food, fuel, and egg colouring.

But the joy of that Easter celebration has remained with me through the decades. At times, the chaos of my life threatens to overwhelm me. It is hard to see how I can keep going. Then I remember Mother and the maxim she lived by: in a world of chaos, find a corner where you still have control and fill it with beauty—then share it with others.

Father, show me how I can bring joy into the lives of all whom I meet today and in so doing bring joy to Your heart also.

Self-Esteem

For it was you who formed my inward parts; you knit me together in my mother's womb.
I praise you, for I am fearfully and wonderfully made.
Wonderful are your works; that I know very well.

PSALM 139:13-14 NSRV

You are neither worm nor wonder but a bundle of possibilities in Jesus Christ.

AUTHOR UNKNOWN

You have made us for Yourself, Lord, and our hearts are restless until they rest in You.

ST. AUGUSTINE OF HIPPO

To say that I am made in the image of God is to say that love is the reason for my existence, for God is love.

THOMAS A KEMPIS

No Outsiders in God's Family

Do you ever feel like an outsider? As if you're on the outside looking in at people having a good time? Yearning so strong it makes your gut ache, overwhelms you. You long to be part of the group, but you're not invited. You turn away engulfed in loneliness and despair, thinking, *Will I ever belong?*

What causes such feelings of isolation, sometimes so all-encompassing that you feel estranged from the whole human race? In my case, the reasons were quite obvious. As a refugee child fleeing from one country to another during the Second World War, I never quite fit in. In the Ukraine and Poland we were hated Germans; in Austria, unwanted refugees; in Canada, new immigrants. Often I wondered, *Who am I really?*

Then too, I felt unwanted and unloved in my own home. I was "different" (how I hated that word!), clumsy in the kitchen, not adept at housework. Because I was the oldest, my overworked mother would sometimes ask me to tend to the wood fire while supper was cooking. With my nose in a book, I would either let the fire go out or feed it too much so that the supper burned. No wonder my mother would scold, "Just get out of the kitchen." So I concluded that I was a burden to her, a nuisance to have around. Throughout the years, I grieved deeply over the inability to please my mother no matter how hard I tried, and I concluded it must be my fault. Later, I transferred my guilt to my marriage when, once more, I couldn't please. Rejection seemed to be my lot.

Into this void stepped Jesus. He let me know that there is one place reserved for me—in His heart. Let me tell you how it happened.

I was fifteen years old then. Two years before that, in September 1949, my mother and four of us children had immigrated to Canada from Europe. These were the days before English as a Second Language (ESL) classes, and we had to learn English the best way we could. In a few months, though, I'd picked up enough of the language to begin high school. But as I ascended the steps of Lord Tweedsmuir High School, my heart was pounding. Would I fit in?

Besides speaking English with a heavy accent, I looked different, with my long braids and hand-me-down clothes. All too soon I discovered a difference that was far more serious: I did not understand Canadian culture, not even the jokes my classmates told me. We'd look at each other blankly, as I was thinking, *Is that supposed to be funny?* Being shy by nature, I pulled back from my classmates by burying myself in my books. In two years, I had not made a single friend.

Gym classes were the worst reminder that I didn't have what it takes. When dance partners or teammates were chosen, the cluster of students around me dwindled as, one by one, their names were called. I knew, of course, why I wasn't chosen. I didn't know how to shoot a basket; I didn't know how to hit a baseball; and I was far too clumsy to be graceful in dancing. I'd be a liability to any team or partner. I wanted to run and hide—I wished the floor would open and mercifully close over me. I wanted to say, "You don't have to choose me if you don't want to. I'll go to the library and read a book." But one couldn't skip gym classes; the teacher would give me to the last team that needed a player.

One day during lunch break, I looked up from the book I was reading and watched two girls talking with their heads together. Such longing rose inside me, I knew I was going to cry. *Oh, to have a friend—just one friend with whom I could talk that way!*

Hurriedly, I left the classroom and hid in the bathroom where I could let the tears fall unnoticed.

Day after day, the same gut-wrenching feeling of loneliness enveloped me. I felt as out of place as a Martian on the wrong planet. Feeling desperately alone, I pushed my way through the crowded halls of Lord Tweedsmuir High School.

After school, I rode the yellow school bus home in silence. I could never think of what to say to the girl beside me. Half an hour later, I stumbled off the bus and hurried into the old farmhouse. As usual, our rented house was empty. Mother, who'd been widowed in the Second World War, worked up to ten hours each day in the vegetable fields to support herself and her four children. Even my siblings weren't home. *They don't have trouble making friends,* I thought. *It's me. Something is very wrong with me.*

Dropping my books on the kitchen table, I ran into the bedroom, slammed the door shut, and fell across the bed. My body, so flat and long and lanky, shook with sobs. I felt I couldn't handle another day of loneliness.

Suddenly, I felt a Presence in the room. I sat up abruptly and looked around but couldn't see anybody. Still, the Presence was palpable—a love so real that I felt hugged. An image burned itself into my mind: a radiant face with friendly eyes that said, "You know what? I *like* you! I've chosen you to be My special friend."

As I sat there on my bed, the gracious words kept coming: "I made you, and you're beautiful to Me. I love you just as you are. I will never leave you nor forsake you."

For a long time I sat there, basking in love beyond my imagining, drinking in words of unconditional acceptance.

When my family members came home, they found me humming as I prepared supper.

The next morning, I opened my eyes to find the joyful Presence still filling the room, as though He'd waited for me to wake up so we could start the day together. When I boarded the yellow bus, He did too. During class, it was as though He were sitting beside me. We did math problems together. We wrote essays together. In gym class, He ran alongside me. At the bus stop, He urged me to get a little closer to the knot of students waiting for the bus. "Listen to them," He seemed to be saying. "Aren't they fun?"

For three glorious months, Jesus walked with me in this almost tangible way. It was as though He were always smiling at me—a big smile of delight and approval—and it was impossible not to smile at others around me. My classmates began to notice. "Helen, you're good in math. Will you help me?" a girl asked. I slid over to make room for her and soon we were studying, heads together. Others invited me to join the glee club. The fact that my classmates now wanted to be with me and offered me their friendship never ceased to amaze me.

Then one dreadful morning I awoke to an empty room. The joyful Presence was gone. *I must have done something terrible to drive him away,* I thought. I confessed every sin I could recall and asked God to forgive me for my unknown sins also. But the palpable sense of His Presence did not return.

Heartbroken, I opened the Bible to search for the words Jesus had spoken to me almost audibly. As I read them over and over, it dawned on me that when Jesus says, "Never will I leave you; never will I forsake you,"[10] He means never. His Presence is just as real, whether I feel it or not. Moreover, His love is real and unchanging, not measured by my moods.

As a shy, clumsy immigrant girl of fifteen, I became aware, in a deeply emotional way, that I am accepted, not because of merit, but because of God's gracious choice. Because He has chosen me, I belong! Then He withdrew the glorious feeling that I might learn to walk by faith. He loved me enough to let me struggle to strengthen the legs of my unsteady faith.

Now when feelings of being an outsider press in upon me—as they sometimes do—I read Jesus' words of affirmation in the Bible over and over: "You did not choose me, but I chose you..."[11] "For he [God] chose us [me] in him [Christ] before the creation of the world...he predestined us [me] to be adopted...in accordance with his pleasure and will."[12]

God says I belong! And feelings have nothing to do with it.

What about you? Have you found this place of belonging? Jesus has reserved a place just for you—in His heart.

The Award Ceremony[13]

Hard work, initiative, determination, and service would finally pay off. Students jostled each other as they flooded the Lord Tweedsmuir High School gym, and the air vibrated with a hum of excited voices. As I followed my classmates to the front section reserved for grads and took a seat near the aisle, I felt a rush of excitement. Awards would be given out for service, sports, scholarships, and the best scholar of the year. I had my hopes set on a scholarship.

Since I'd been in the top five of the class academically all year, my teacher had encouraged me to apply. "You've done extremely well in your second language," the teacher said.

Some of my classmates agreed. "If anybody deserves to get it, you do," they said.

My spine tingled as I envisioned my crowning moment: shaking hands with the principal, getting my picture taken, listening to the clapping, seeing the grinning faces of my friends.

I was sorry that nobody from my family was able to come to the awards ceremony. But my family had moved to another town, and I had gone to live with friends. My mother understood that I wanted to graduate with my class, and, of course, I didn't want anything to come between me and the scholarship.

I looked up at the stage framed by two flags, the Canadian maple leaf and the provincial rising sun over the Pacific ocean. On the stage sat Mr. Brown—our principal—several teachers, and dignitaries. A master of ceremonies stepped up to the mike, welcomed everyone, and announced the national anthem. As the band began to play "O Canada," the students rose and stood at attention.

After the song, we listened to the usual boring speeches, and then the master of ceremonies moved over to a table of plaques, trophies, and scrolls tied with ribbons. "The time has come that we've all been waiting for," he said. "In pursuit of excellence, it is fitting that we honour hard work and perseverance. Many students in this assembly have made our school proud, and it gives me great pleasure to acknowledge each of them publicly." My heart swelled at his gracious words. "When I call your name, would you please come forward and receive your award?"

It seemed to take forever for the students from the lower grades to receive their awards, but, clapping enthusiastically, I was happy for them. The closer it came to our class, though, the more excited I became. I just hoped that on the way up to the platform, I wouldn't trip on a cord or something. Well, I'd watch it.

It wasn't as if I'd never been on the stage before. With hard work and prayer, I'd been on the honour roll each year, but this year would be the first time I'd ever received a scholarship. I needed the money to carry on with my higher education. Being the oldest in our family, I couldn't expect any financial help from my widowed mother, who was struggling just to put food on the table. But more than the money, I needed a tangible "well done" for having worked hard to achieve my high school education in a second language.

My mind drifted back five years to my first day in a Canadian school. Even though I was thirteen years old, because I didn't speak any English I was placed in the grade three classroom with children half my size. The children didn't seem to care that I was as tall as their teacher. They swarmed around me, offering smiles and crayons and instructions. They must have thought Heidi from the Swiss Alps had come to class when they saw me wearing thick, blonde braids, a starched pinafore, and woolen stockings. I could have played the game by telling them I lived with my uncle, except I didn't know how to say it in English. All I could do was smile and receive their gifts.

So, on that first day, I squeezed into a small desk and coloured squares with objects in them. Carefully I repeated the words underneath each square: "cow," "dog," "cat," "girl..." My teacher gave me a reader to take home. I looked up key words in a German-English dictionary, then wrote them on a piece of paper with the definition beside each. After I folded the paper over, I would guess what each word meant. Each day, my vocabulary grew. How excited I was when I could actually pick out words in conversations and catch the gist of what the teacher and my classmates were saying. Day after day, I began to understand more and, what was even more amazing, they began to understand me.

In six months, my teacher felt I was ready for high school. But I was scared. My English was still pretty rusty, and coming into grade seven at the end of February, I'd be way behind my classmates. I'd feel really stupid.

But to my surprise, my high school classmates accepted me and never, ever laughed at me or my crazy answers. I always cringed when the teacher asked us to exchange papers. Often I guessed at the questions, and I guessed even more at the answers.

I studied my textbooks every chance I had, during lunch break, after school, and in the evening. I drilled in vocabulary and pronunciation. It took me months to learn to position my tongue just right so I could say the difficult "th" sound. I studied my pocket dictionary even more than my Bible. When I passed grade seven, I was jubilant.

As my English improved, my studies became easier. But I never let up studying; I loved learning and the challenge of good grades. *A scholarship will be a great climax to finishing high school*, I thought.

"And now, our grade twelve graduates," the master of ceremonies announced, bringing my thoughts back to the assembly. I felt a shiver go through me. This was the moment I'd been waiting for. First came the awards for participation in clubs, good citizenship, and sports, and then the scholarships. My cheeks burned and my heart raced as I listened to name after name being called. One after another of my classmates walked across the stage, shook the hands of the principal and the person giving the award, stopped for a moment to grin into a camera, and then stepped aside to join the others. There was wild clapping and cheering. I clapped along with the rest, but I began to feel uneasy. Why wasn't my name called? *Don't worry, your turn will come*, I told myself.

But my name was not called. My turn never came.

Disappointment crashed upon me, leaving me dazed. *What happened?*

My mind in a turmoil, I hardly heard the master of ceremony announce that now the honour rolls would be given out. *It's small comfort for not getting a scholarship*, I thought bitterly, *but at least it's something*. As names of deserving classmates were called, they rose to their feet. I tensed to jump up too, but again, my name was not called. As I watched my friends walk across the platform to receive a scroll tied with a ribbon, not even the loud clapping drowned out the turmoil in my head. *No honour roll!* I was stunned. I'd been receiving an honour roll for the past four years. I was in the top five in my class! Then why wasn't my name called?

The assembly ended. Students congregated around the winners to congratulate them. Some posed while a friend or parent took their photo. I hurried outside to get a grip on my emotions.

I'd been so sure of getting a scholarship and even more sure of an honour roll. But I had received nothing.

Totally devastated, I walked to the school office. My heart pounded in my temples as I asked to see the principal. I'd never asked to see him before, but now I had to find out what went wrong.

As I walked into Mr Brown's office, he rose from his chair, all six feet four inches of him, and looked down into my flushed face. "Yes, Helen. What is it you want?"

"I didn't get a scholarship," I said.

He studied his hands for a moment. "You certainly qualified for a scholarship," he said slowly. "But unfortunately you forfeited it by choosing to go to a Bible school instead of a secular school."

"There was no honour roll either," I choked.

Mr. Brown's eyebrows shot up in surprise. He rummaged around on his desk for a moment, then found a scroll with a ribbon tied around it. My honour roll. For some reason, it had not been put into the box that was carried onto the stage. Now he handed it to me. "Well, here you are," he said.

My cheeks burned with humiliation. My throat constricted. The office furniture blurred.

I snatched the honour roll, turned on my heels, and fled from the principal's office.

I fought tears all the way home on the yellow school bus. Back at the farm where I was boarding, I hid behind a barn where nobody would find me. I couldn't let my friends see me cry. I couldn't bear to hear them say, "What's the big deal? You passed grade twelve, didn't you?"

I flopped down on the grass. *What's the good of hard work, year after year, when nobody cares. Nobody ever says, "I'm proud of you."*

I kept seeing, like a video in slow motion, myself sitting in a gym amidst other anxious students. Straining to hear my name called. Waiting to be asked to come forward. Waiting for the applause. Instead, nothing. A big zero.

Suddenly, into my mind's eye flashed a vivid scene. I saw Jesus sitting in the bleachers of the gymnasium. He stood up and smiled at me. Then He called my name, slowly and distinctly. "Helen, come forward."

As I walked towards Him, I heard applause. Jesus was clapping for me, and it seemed as if all the people sitting in the bleachers with Him were clapping for me, too. "I've seen your hard work." He spoke the words directly into my heart. "I've recorded it in My book."

As His words washed over me, a warm comfort enveloped me. A quietness settled on my spirit. A glow of satisfaction replaced the turmoil in my heart.

During the days and weeks that followed, when a memory of the humiliating assembly returned, I'd hear Jesus whisper, "You did great. I believe in you."

In time, my wounded spirit healed and I was able to forget about my disappointment. But I've never forgotten the wonderful feeling when I saw Jesus standing in ovation for me.

I realize now what a great gift Jesus gave me that day. Instead of a scholarship that is temporal, He gave me the comfort of His Holy Spirit, which stays forever. The Holy Spirit made Jesus real, so real that I can still hear Him cheering me on. He picks me up when I'm down. He gives me courage to do my best, even when nobody is watching.

It's great to be on Jesus's honour roll.

God Uses Nobodies

How does a person voted least likely to succeed in life become an international award winning journalist? Read on.

I watched my teacher, short and stout with tight black curly hair, cross the street and approach our house. My heart began to beat louder. What did she want? Was she coming to tell my mother about the strapping I got in front of the class with everyone looking on and smirking? I still cringed at the humiliation. My teacher never smiled. She hardly ever spoke to me, and when she did, I felt demeaned.

"Well, Mrs. T, do come in," my mother said. She served tea in Royal Albert china cups and delicious *speculaas*. I hovered in the distance. The teacher adjusted her wire-rimmed glasses over a sharp nose and came to the point of her visit. "Trudy is a slow learner, you see. When she came into my class she couldn't count past ten, and she couldn't tell colours." She made a face as though this were a serious deficiency. "She's learned to read, but she's poor in arithmetic," she continued. "We'll pass her on condition. But I came to warn you, your daughter may have a hard time in grade two."

"We speak too much Dutch at home," my mother said. "From now on, I'll talk more English to her. And I'll drill her in figures." Thus the two talked about me as though I were invisible.

I'm ugly, dumb! Once more I'd heard the verdict. Throughout my school years, in many different ways, this label was drilled into me until I began to believe it.

One day a group of kids had gathered on the playground around a student who was blind. I joined them and saw that Darlene had covered her eyes with both hands.

"Hey, Trudy, look at this," Kenneth said as he extended his hand.

"What?"

"It's Darlene's eye." A small round object, brown and glistening in the sun, lay in the palm of his hand. The kids around Kenneth were also gazing at the "eye."

I was horrified, and my mouth dropped open. "Darlene's eye fell out!" I blurted.

Suddenly everyone was laughing uproariously. "It's a marble, you dummy."

"Lazy-eye Trudy is so dumb," they jeered.

Blushing crimson, I covered my left eye, smaller than the right. Although I'd had surgery on the eye muscles, my eye still looked droopy. Add to this scraggly hair that stuck out all over and a continuous runny nose from allergies. Not only was I dumb, I was ugly to boot. The bell rang and we returned to the classroom.

I had little interest in what was happening in class. Gazing out the window, I watched the birds playing in the trees. I desperately wanted to be home on our tulip farm, roaming the countryside with my brothers or playing in the woods by Beaver Creek.

The great outdoors fascinated me. I caught honeybees with my bare hands, climbed trees and studied butterfly cocoons, made an aquarium for salamanders, and watched the frogs and salmon in the stream. Trees. Streams. Insects. Birds. And books. These were my friends.

I read everything, from comics and newspapers to science textbooks. One Christmas, I begged my mother and father to buy me *The Living World of Science* and *The Living World of Nature,* two red, large, hard-covered encyclopedias written for kids. I learned about bees and flowers and electricity. I also got to know scientists like Albert Einstein, Thomas Edison, and Leonardo da Vinci.

Unfortunately, none of this mattered in a classroom setting. Although by age twelve I had caught up with the rest of the class and my eye looked almost normal, thanks to muscle strengthening exercises, the label stuck: "Lazy-eye Trudy is so dumb."

My teen years plunged me into a hellish nightmare. My father demanded complete and instant obedience, and when I didn't give it to him, he'd fly into a rage. He beat me mercilessly, pulled my hair, and knocked out two of my teeth. I could never be sure when I'd provoke another attack of his anger. Yet my brothers didn't receive this kind of treatment. My mother also seemed to favour the boys. Feeling I had nobody to support me, I turned to alcohol and drugs.

During one LSD trip I was overwhelmed with horrible hallucinations. In a full-colour choreographed horror movie, menacing cartoon characters leered at me. For five long hours they screamed angry words as they reached for me, almost grabbing me. Terrified, I lay on my bed sobbing and shaking. I would have gone mad, except for a quiet voice that kept repeating, "Your mother loves you; your father loves you; and God loves you." Like a trickle of cool water, the words washed over my feverish brain, whispering hope. Finally I calmed down and sanity was restored. This experience scared me enough to quit hard drugs. But it took a whole year of intense struggle before I was able to leave hashish and marijuana.

Then something wonderful happened: a young man showed an interest in me. Larry treated me with kindness and courtesy. Being noticed was such a novel feeling. When Larry told me that he loved me and wanted to marry me, I accepted gladly. *If someone can love me like that, maybe I am worth something*, I thought.

After high school graduation, Larry and I were married. A year later, we had a baby girl. In time we had two more children. Looking into the faces of my beautiful daughters, I was overwhelmed with the privilege and wonder of being a mother.

Larry and I bought an office cleaning business, and I became a cleaning lady. I loved the actual work of cleaning offices, the interaction with the secretaries, and the fact that I had a paying job that allowed me to be home with the kids when they were home from school. I figured I'd reached the pinnacle of success.

But more than that, I'd found God, and He'd found me. In reading the Bible, I'd heard Jesus' wonderful invitation: "My sheep listen to my voice; I know them, and they follow me. I give them eternal life, and they shall never perish; no one can snatch them out of my hand."[14] As though He were calling my name, I'd heard Jesus calling me. Me! The girl who had so little to offer! I knew I didn't deserve God's love; still Jesus had loved me enough to die for me. Such love was beyond my imagining. Weeping, I gave my heart to Christ, and He inundated me with His love. Like a seed that's been lying in the ground waiting for resurrection, I felt the stirring of new life within me. Like a person stumbling out of darkness into light, I began to see new truths.

Each morning as I read the Bible—hungrily soaking up its words—I was overwhelmed afresh by God's love for me. I saw that I was no accident but made in God's image according to His divine blueprint. "Now God is shining in our hearts to let you know that his glory is seen in Jesus Christ. We are like clay jars in which this treasure is stored. The real power comes from God and not from us."[15] I certainly felt liked a blemished jar of clay; yet according to God's word, the wonderful treasure of Jesus was within me. This never ceased to amaze me.

After a few years Larry wanted a change of career. Not knowing what to do next, he went to seek the advice of our pastor, who was also a psychologist. While he was talking to him, I was milling about in the foyer, waiting for him so we could go home together.

Suddenly the pastor called me into the office. "Trudy, I'm about to give your husband an aptitude test," he said."Why don't you take it too?"

"Me? Why?"

"The price is the same," he smiled.

I shook my head no. *No way do I want to show you how dumb I am,* I thought.

But the pastor persisted, and I took the test. When the results came back, I was totally shocked. Creativity and intelligence were at the top.

"You've given me somebody else's test results," I stammered.

"No, this is you." He smiled. "You could be a doctor or a lawyer, Trudy," the pastor said softly.

I went home, hurried to my bedroom, sat down on my bed, and studied the results again. Disbelief gave way to depression. *If this is true, why didn't one of my teachers or some adult in my life pick up on it?* I thought angrily. *What good does it do me now? At twenty-eight years I'm too old to become a doctor or a lawyer.*

"Jesus, show me what you want me to do."I prayed.

He answered, not with a vision, but with a whisper, a desire to go to university.

On the first day, as I stepped into a classroom, I almost turned on my heels and ran. In my mind's eye I saw again the disdaining look of a teacher and heard again the jeering voices of fellow classmates and my mother's warning, "Forget it, Trudy. You'll never make it."

I took a deep breath and whispered, "I can do everything through [Christ] who gives me strength."[16] Fortified by those words, I went inside. Soon I was loving everything to do with learning: the interaction with other students, the research, and soaking up new information.

About midway during my pursuit of an English degree, I chose to study journalism. Why journalism? I'm not sure. Since very young I had dabbled in the mystery and wonder of words and poetry. But I didn't, for one moment, believe that I had the gift of writing. I simply prayed daily for wisdom to do God's will. Students at the college recognized my talent before I did. They chose me to be the editor of the college newspaper.

Now, fifteen years later, by God's grace and kindness, I've received twenty-one provincial, national, and international awards, plus two Jack Webster awards. I'm shocked by the sheer number of awards, because, really, who am I that I should receive such recognition? I'm the slow learner. The cleaning lady. The person least likely to succeed.

Still, God chose me to demonstrate His grace and power. He's raised me up to more than I could imagine in my wildest dream. He'll do the same for you. Trust Him.

Editor's note: In the past year alone Trudy has won ten awards. Among them:

Three first place awards in the Suburban Newspaper Association of America, which represents more than 2,000 newspapers in Canada and the U.S.A. They are: Best News Story, Best Environmental Series and Best In-depth Reporting.

Three first place national awards from the Canadian Community Newspaper Association for Best News Story, Best Feature Story, and Best Business Story.

Two first place awards from the B.C. Yukon Newspaper Association

One Jack Webster award and the Golden Rooster for Agriculture coverage.

Gems of Truth: A New Identity

"Therefore, if anyone is in Christ, he is a new creation; the old has gone, the new has come! All this is from God, who reconciled us to himself through Christ."[17]

Linda came from an abusive family. She had been physically abused by her father and verbally abused by her mother. Consequently, she had very low self-esteem, which often sabotaged her best efforts. *I'm programmed to be a loser,* she thought. *How can I possibly be anything else?* She lived in defeat and despair.

Then Linda learned about Jesus Christ, how He'd come to save us from sin and the damaging effects of sin. Hope began to whisper that she could be set free from her sin and the negative influences of her past. She gave her life to Christ. She began to read God's Word and apply it to her heart.

When negative voices clamoured for attention, she would counter, "In Christ, I am a new creation; the old has gone, the new has come!" She wrote Scripture verses, like the above, on cards that she would carry with her while driving the car or going on walks. Again and again, she would repeat God's truths out loud, adding, "That's my new identity." When failure threatened to overwhelm her, she'd say, "I don't have to stay down. If the risen Lord Jesus Christ is living within me, then I have the power to rise again." And depending totally upon God, she did rise—again and again.

As she fed on God's truths day after day, month after month, and year after year, her self-esteem grew. She began to see that it's not what has happened to us in the past but our belief system at the present—what we believe about God and ourselves—that determines success or failure. Success is not mind over matter but truth over error.

Thank you, Father, that You have chosen me to be Your child.

Marriage

Lord, help us to remember when first we met,
the strong love that grew between us,
And to work that love into practical things
So nothing can divide us.
We ask for words both kind and loving
and for hearts always ready to ask forgiveness
as well as to forgive.
Dear Lord, we put our marriage into your hands.

AUTHOR UNKNOWN

If I have a faith that can move mountains, but have not
love, I am nothing.

1 CORINTHIANS 13:2

Love is a work in progress. Love gives a sizable piece of
time we think we can't spare.

ARDIS WHITMAN[18]

The best relationship is one in which your love for each
other exceeds your need for each other.

AUTHOR UNKNOWN

Leaning Into the Curves[19]

I heard my husband's motorcycle roar out of the driveway of our home. *Another holiday alone,* I thought bitterly. It was July 1, and Tony, my fifty-nine-year-old husband, would be spending this gloriously sunny Dominion Day (Canada's Independence Day) motor-biking with friends from church.

"At the age of fifty-three," I had warned him, "I'm not about to start riding a motorbike! People will wonder, 'What's that grey-haired woman doing on the back of a bike?' Besides, it is a cold, dangerous, and stupid thing to do." Staring at the back of my husband's neck and helmet was not my idea of seeing the scenery. Besides, I'd be freezing and too miserable to enjoy the lush farmlands and the magnificent views of our British Columbia.

I stormed into the garage, which I had made into a sewing room for my drapery business, and I began to cut fabric. All day my machine whirred furiously as I simmered out loud. "Last weekend, he took off to the west for Victoria, and this weekend he's gone south to Mount Baker. Where will he be *next* weekend?"

Mount Baker, with its snow-capped peak, was perfect for a summer outing. It was only an hour's drive away. I checked my watch. By now, they were probably having lunch on the mountain.

"He could at least have asked me to go along!" Angrily I yanked a piece of material from the machine. "It would have given me the pleasure of turning him down."

We used to spend our weekends and holidays together. The thought filled my eyes with tears. Tony and I were both from German Mennonite homes in the plains of Saskatchewan. I was eighteen and he was twenty-three when we married, and in the thirty-six years since then, we had shared not only four wonderful children but also many intimate times—long nature drives, Sunday visits with close friends, and gardening sessions among the rows of organically grown vegetables and herbs in our yard.

In 1965, we moved to a four-acre strawberry farm in Abbotsford, where Tony worked as a mechanic and I worked as a drapery maker. Then, after moving to town, we each started our own business: Tony had his driving school, and I fashioned draperies.

Over the years, we'd grown so compatible that words oftentimes weren't necessary. Just the touch of a hand, or a smile, or simply a look meant we were having a lovely time. We enjoyed being together, at least until recently.

I had tried to discourage Tony from buying a motorbike, but he'd gone ahead and bought it anyway. Initially, our teenage sons had been the ones to influence their dad into motorbiking. But they were grown now, and their dad had just gone out and bought a powerful bike for himself. Ridiculous!

It's forcing a wedge between us, I thought resentfully.

I was banging away in the kitchen, throwing supper together, when Tony rumbled up and parked in front of the house. Sunburned and bright-eyed from his ride, he tried to tell me about the day. "What a super time..." he began. But my look warned him to keep silent. I was too hurt to trust myself to speak.

Day by day, I nursed my self-pity. Tony tried to reason with me. "Give it at least one try, Anne." Tony, the big, strong, silent one, eyed me anxiously, but I gave him the cold shoulder. His gentle pleading annoyed me and made me feel guilty.

He would leave for his driver-training school, and I would bury my angry self in the business of shaping yards of material into decorative window hangings. I used to love sewing, but now it seemed like sheer drudgery. It became just a job, and I went through the motions mechanically while anguishing over the trouble between Tony and me. I wanted that bike off the yard, and the sooner he got the message, the better.

Evenings became strained. Meals were eaten in forced silence. Afterwards, Tony would busy himself in the garden or work alone in the darkroom on a photography project. And without a look or a word in his direction, I would return to my sewing room.

I'm usually a happy person, but now resentment and jealousy consumed me. After three weeks of this ugly pattern, I was miserable. A heavy spirit of sadness left me feeling drained, lifeless.

Seven years earlier, Jesus had become very real to me. I'd felt alive and full of joy. Like two close friends, the Lord and I had kept in touch as the sewing machine hummed away at my work. At that time, I had rejoiced in the words of King David: "You have made known to me the path of life; you will fill me with joy in your presence, with eternal pleasures at your right hand."[20] And I had always longed for some way to pass that message on to others.

Now, though, reading those words failed to bring me joy or comfort. God, too, was silent, distant.

At the sewing machine that day, I wondered aloud, "What's happening to me?" The work in front of me blurred as tears streamed down my cheeks. *There's no fun in life. There's no fun in me. I'm a bitter old woman, the kind I vowed I would never become.*

The thought terrified me. Alarmed, I sat down on a chair and sobbed to the Lord.

"I can't stand it any more. Either make Tony hate riding that bike or make me love it, but let us be together in this for Your glory."

Sitting there, feeling desolate, I wondered whether God was listening any more. Would He answer? All my senses were alert, waiting, but the only thing I was aware of was the radio playing softly on my cutting table.

The next weekend dawned sunny and clear. "Anne," Tony asked kindly, "would you like to go to the Minter Gardens with me?"

These were magnificent formal gardens with sculpted hedges and flowers laid out in elaborate designs. They had recently been opened to the public, and yes, I wanted very much to visit them. But they were an hour's drive from home.

"By car?"

"No," Tony said sheepishly, "I thought we'd take the bike."

Then, after a slight hesitation, I heard these incredible words coming out of my mouth: "Okay, I'll go. But what should I wear?"

A sparkle came into Tony's eyes. "Something warm," he replied. "Be sure to wear two pairs of slacks."

Two pairs of slacks weren't enough. Neither were the extra sweaters and jacket. As the scenery sped past, I clung to Tony and shivered in the cold. The bike roared beneath us.

"Relax," Tony encouraged. "Lean into the curves with me."

Awkwardly at first, I tried to synchronize my body movements with his. Then, as we harmonized more and more, my heart swelled with joy to feel the togetherness, to feel the freedom. It was like riding the wind. And it didn't seem to matter that my curls were grey, nor that I was fifty-three, nor that my husband with his receding hairline was nearly sixty.

As the cold caught at me, I smiled at God. "Are You cold, too?" I asked. How natural it felt to be talking with Him on friendly terms again.

That bike I hated actually brought me back together with Jesus. Today, I have a Honda CB 650cc. Tony and I have joined the International Christian Bikers Association, which gives us a chance to study and pray with other bikers and to pass along His message at rallies, even to those bikers who call themselves Hell's Angels.

And if anyone asks me, "What's a grey-haired woman like you doing on a motorbike?" I simply reply, "I'm having the time of my life!"

Anne Dueck

Gems of Truth: Eyes of Grace[21]

Sheila and I just celebrated our thirtieth wedding anniversary. Somebody asked her, what was our secret? She answered, "On my wedding day, I decided to make a list of ten of Tim's faults that, for the sake of our marriage, I would always overlook. I figured I could live with at least ten."

When she was asked which faults she had listed, Sheila replied, "I never did get around to listing them. Instead, every time he does something that makes me mad, I simply say to myself, "Lucky for him, it's one of the ten."

My Husband Has AIDS[22]

I'm a lively person who wants to live each moment intensely. Perhaps that's why in my dating years I was strongly attracted to Christian men with whom I could do activities such as hiking, skiing and riding.

Then I met Brad. A hemophiliac from birth, he'd spent much of his life in hospitals. Yet his zest for living and delightful sense of humour drew me to him. Moreover, his depth of character and accepting attitude of all of life—the good and the bad—exuded a healing quality that I found very refreshing.

I fell deeply in love with him and couldn't possibly be totally realistic about marriage. Yet I tried to understand what it would mean to marry Brad: frequent hospitalizations for him, more manual labour for me, fewer sports, and more quiet activities for both of us.

Both of us loved the Lord and felt He had led us together. He would help us make the necessary adjustments to each other. We married nine years ago when I was twenty. We had two children and dreamed of a long, happy life together.

The news that hemophiliacs are prime candidates for getting AIDS (Acquired Immune Deficiency Syndrome) hit us like a bombshell. We read everything we could get our hands on and attended seminars. When some of our hemophiliac friends tested positive for HIV (the AIDS virus), we became even more alarmed. What about Brad?

Since infancy, he'd needed blood transfusions. Even now he gives himself one a week. Each bottle of serum, containing the clotting factor, has been made up from blood given by about 100 donors. Because strict screening methods to obtain blood are a relatively new thing, it was highly probable Brad had been infected with the virus.

Should he get tested? His doctor advised, "No. Why burden yourself? Think about the implications. The prejudice. The fear. Wouldn't you rather be able to say, 'I don't know?' Take the necessary precautions, but apart from that, live as normally as you can."

But Brad is a realist. He wanted to know for sure. Maybe he did it for my sake, so he could protect me. Anyway, he was tested.

When he showed me the paper with the positive HIV on it, neither of us said much. I told my parents, and they said they'd pray for us. But beyond that, we didn't talk about it. I think we were trying to protect each other from hurt. Maybe it was also denial. Anything as horrible as AIDS couldn't happen to us. We were young and had just begun our lives together.

For a while, we didn't do anything about our situation. But soon every time I heard the word AIDS, it struck terror into my heart. The stories I'd given intellectual assent to now became emotion packed and frightening.

When Brad bought a box of condoms, anger seized me. Even this very private part of our world had been invaded by fear. What had once been so enjoyable became a threatening thing, something that could kill me too. Deeply hurt and confused, I railed at God, "Why do You let your people get so hurt? Why didn't You protect us?"

Tension grew between Brad and me. He spent more and more time in his office. I kept an emotional distance from him, thinking, *If I stop being so feminine, he won't desire me.* After all, I had to protect myself.

Months went by. Finally, after watching a particularly disturbing documentary on AIDS, Brad approached me on the subject. I discovered his fears were not for himself but for me and the children. He wanted to keep providing for us, to give us all a normal life. Not knowing how much time he had left, he felt driven to work overtime. He felt deeply frustrated about not being able to offer us a more secure future.

I told him that the future scared me as well. If he died, I would not only lose my best friend but also the provider for our family. I didn't have a vocation or training, and Brad couldn't get life insurance. How would I support myself and our two children? Knowing I could be infected, who would want to marry me?

We held each other and tried to pray.

After Brad had gone to sleep, I tossed beside him for hours, too tortured by fear to be able to sleep. Fear for Brad, the children, myself.

"Lord Jesus, You have the power to heal. You've healed other people; why don't You heal my husband?" I cried.

"Cast out fear." The voice of Jesus was clear and definite, obviously not a suggestion but a command. He seemed to be saying, "Before I can do anything for you, you must cast out fear. It does not come from Me."

My heart still pounding, I prayed, "In the name of Jesus, I bind all my fears about the AIDS virus and our uncertain future and cast them out." Immediately, a deep peace flooded my spirit. It was as though Jesus were right there in the room with me.

"Look to Me," He continued speaking, "not to other people's miracles. What I do with your life is my personal love gift to you. I will never leave you nor forsake you."

Almost three years have passed since that night, and Brad's hospitalizations are more frequent now. And at times

I am afraid, but it's not the terrorizing, paralyzing fear it once was.

We've been able to talk about it to our friends and church family, and most of them have been supportive. But some people's questions convey a morbid curiosity, like a small boy poking at a dead cat.

I want people to talk to the Lord about us, to really pray. Sometimes I need to spout off. "Look, I'm scared. I'm angry. I'm frustrated. I'm tired of having to pray for my husband." I need to feel I'm accepted in spite of my negative emotional outbursts.

Sometimes we feel guilty for letting this adversity in our lives affect us so deeply, yet to deny our honest emotions would not be truthful. We do grieve. We do hurt. We are scared. We need emotional support.

Sometimes, people ask me if I think Brad is going to be healed. I don't know. I don't have a promise of healing from the Lord. What He gave me that night was His peace and a deep assurance that no matter what happens, He'll always look after us in love. Certainly God has the power to heal, but I don't know God's agenda.

I've learned there are two ways of looking at any situation: with eyes that are being educated by the world and its statistics or with eyes that see the Lord and His truths.

Knowing the Faithful One—the sovereign God who loves us with an everlasting love—enables us to live life fully in the present. We're a boisterous family and have a lot of fun together. Whatever the future holds, I know we will be cared for.

Jennifer Brown

When Life is Unfair[23]

O ne of the quickest ways for me to lose my joy is to compare my life with the lives of others. God has blessed me with five wonderful children, my own home (small but paid for), a solid family nearby, many friends, and rewarding ministries. I'm content with my life—until I look across the fence and see what my neighbour has!

We may laugh at this, but it can be disquieting. Take, for instance, a banquet I attended recently.

The hotel foyer buzzed with smartly dressed people. "So good to see you," friends greeted each other. Then came the time for us to take our places at the tables. As couples waved to other couples to sit with them, the Tempter whispered to me, "And where is your husband? Don't you deserve to be blessed like the others here?"

Truth is, our marriage had ended in divorce. After years of anguish, I thought I had adjusted by accepting my situation and focusing my thoughts on present blessings. But in the midst of all these happy couples, doubts nibbled at my joy. I struggled with thoughts like *God isn't really fair, is He? He's holding back a blessing from me.*

Later I pondered: if we lived in a world where everybody enjoyed the same blessings, then we wouldn't need to compare. We'd all bask in God's goodness, content with what He has given us.

Then I remembered Eve. She lived in a perfect world, enjoyed a perfect marriage, and walked in perfect harmony with God. What more could she have wanted? But the

Tempter said to her, "You lack one thing. You don't have the knowledge of good and evil. If you had this, think how much happier you'd be. You would be like God."[24] Doubting the goodness of God got Eve into trouble.

When I compare what I have to what others have, I am doubting God's goodness in my life. The apostle Paul wrote, "Those who compare are not wise."[25] Comparisons shift my focus away from God onto my circumstances, spawning thoughts of discontent.

When I'm tempted to doubt God's goodness, it helps me to consider what God is like. The most complete picture of God that we have is Jesus Christ: "The Son is the radiance of God's glory and the exact representation of his being."[26] During His time on earth, Jesus was God dressed in humanity.

Did Jesus suffer unfairness in His earthly life? Did He lack good things? Knowing why Jesus lived and died—the grand plan of salvation God worked out for us—I can say, "But Jesus had to suffer these things. It was all part of the plan."

What about me? Shouldn't I conclude that God has a plan for my life as well and that the unfairness I suffer may be part of it?

God is fair. Life is not. We err when we measure the goodness of God by the rightness of our circumstances.

A few years ago, my mother's brother from Russia visited us in Canada. During his life Uncle Peter had suffered in the purges of Russia and in a labour camp in Siberia. He had barely escaped with his life. After his release, he had returned to his village, but he had found nobody waiting for him there. His wife had remarried. His house had been destroyed in the war. He had no possessions. Life in Russia, even as a free man, was a constant struggle for survival.

My mother took Uncle Peter to visit a friend whom he had known in the old country but had immigrated to

Canada before Stalin's reign of terror. The friend, a prosperous farmer, welcomed his old school chum warmly and asked him to enter his home. Uncle Peter stared with open-mouthed wonder at the lovely surroundings, rooms filled with elegant furniture and modern appliances. Then his friend gave him a tour of his farm. As Uncle Peter saw the long chicken barns, farm equipment, and rich farmland, he was overcome with confusion. How could one man own so much? With a sweep of his arm, his Canadian friend remarked, "God has been good to me, as you can see."

At the time, propriety kept Uncle Peter from commenting, but later he blurted out his frustration to my mother, "And what about me? Doesn't God love me, too?"

The Bible teaches that God's goodness is rooted in His character; His goodness is the same whether our circumstances are good or bad.[27] God's love for the Canadian farmer and Uncle Peter is the same.

When I compare myself with others (as I did at the banquet), I remind myself of God's love. God loves me! Whatever happens, God always acts in love towards me. Knowing this makes it easier for me to see my own blessings. I focus on what I have, not on what I don't have. And I trust my loving God with the rest.

Motherhood

No other success in life—
not being president,
or being wealthy, or going
to college, or writing
a book, or anything else—
comes up to the success
of the man or woman who
can feel that they have
done their duty and that
their children
and grandchildren rise up
and call them blessed.

THEODORE ROOSEVELT, 1917

A hundred years from now it will not matter what my
bank account was, the sort of house I lived in, or the
kind of car I drove... But the world may be different
because I was important in the life of a child.

AUTHOR UNKNOWN

Making Memories[28]

I felt trapped.

In a drafty old house, legally condemned, at the edge of town. Five acres of an abandoned orchard, a cornfield, and a freeway between us and the neighbours.

A mountain of dirty laundry on the kitchen floor. Diapers churning in the old wringer washer. I shut off the machine and lifted a handful of dripping laundry to feed through the wringer. It squealed pitifully but refused to budge. Broken again!

Children squabbled in the bedroom. I ran to see and tripped over building blocks and cars, dolls and stuffed animals that littered the floor.

"Clean up this mess," I thundered. Instantly, I regretted my harsh tone. Both children had colds again. They picked up everything going: colds, influenza, chicken pox, mumps, and complications with mumps. Add to that the usual childhood accidents. I kept running to the emergency room, nerve-racking at all times but especially now, since we had no medical coverage.

I picked up baby Lisa, age one and a half, wiped her nose and held her close as I stared outside. Esther, age seven, would soon be home for lunch. A driving rain pelted the window. I hoped she had remembered her boots.

If only my husband were home; he would know what to do with the washing machine. But he was boarding with friends in the city and attending university all week. Since he needed our family car, it left me without transportation for the week.

Not that it mattered a great deal. I had nowhere to go and no money to spend. It was a struggle to put food on the table. Of course there wasn't any money for appliance repairs. I would have to wring the clothes by hand and hang them over chairs near the heater in the living room to dry.

I held my hand over the oil heater, our only source of heat in the house. Out again. Extinguished by the wind. No wonder it was so cold in this house.

I sat Lisa on the floor, and she promptly began to howl. "David, come play with Lisa," I yelled to our four-year-old.

Kneeling on the cold linoleum floor, I lit a match and fumbled to find the place underneath the oil heater to light it. The match went out.

Now David's angry voice joined the baby's fretful crying.

My emotional dam broke. Tears spilled over my cheeks. How much more could I take of this bedlam: always scrounging to make ends meet; keeping sick, cooped-up kids happy in a drafty, old place; cleaning endlessly and never arriving at a neat and tidy house.

I sat up and blew my nose, feeling suddenly ashamed. What had happened to my resolve to be a happy mother of children? *Perhaps when the kids are older and life is tidier*, I thought. *Now all I can hope for is survival.*

To help with finances, I went to work one day a week at a senior care home while my mother looked after the children. She enjoyed playing with her grandchildren and I welcomed the reprieve. I loved nursing seniors. I could learn so much from them, I figured, listening to their stories and seeing how they had coped with challenges in their lives. How true that proved to be!

One day, I stopped to see old Mrs. Bartel, a frail woman suffering from dementia, who most of the time chattered senselessly. But on this day, she surprised me. Wanting to make conversation, I pointed to a photograph of an old farmhouse hanging on her bare wall.

"Was this your house?" I asked.

"Yes," she smiled. "Children loved to swing from the tree." She pointed to a rubber tire suspended from a huge cedar tree beside the veranda. "Children ran in and out of the house, slamming the door." She chuckled at the memory. "I served them juice and cookies on the veranda. They liked my jam-jams the best." Bright sparkles lit up her brown eyes, shining with the memory." Those were happy times," she patted my hand. "You know, dear, good days." She was perfectly lucid now, chatting happily of a time in her life when her children were small. With a start I realized, *She's talking about my time.*

I left her room, wondering at the marvel of selective memory. In her bleak, senile days, Mrs. Bartel seemed to have forgotten many important life events, but the memory of a houseful of small children pierced through her confusion like a shining star. Perhaps, of all the times in our lives, this *was* the most enduring. Maybe these frantic days were really the most important the children and I had. If so, how could I be more intentional about making them memorable?

The following morning, deliberately putting housework aside, I took the children on a nature hike past the cornfield and into a park. We played by the creek and picked buttercups. I pushed the children on a swing. When we returned home, I pulled a coffee table over and said, "Put your nature treasures here. This will be our show-and-tell table." Soon bits of moss, smooth stones, pieces of coloured glass, fresh flowers, and bottle caps adorned the table.

Oh, the housework still had to be done, but now something else took first place. Many times I'd ask myself, "What will the children and I remember ten years from now? My tidy house, or the fun we had doing something together?" So we set out to make family fun each day. We discovered a fort in an abandoned apple tree. We made up silly little songs about the dog, like, "Brandy dog, Brandy dog, don't be like a frog, hopping in my garden and squishing all the plants." We rolled dough into lopsided buns or cut out sugar cookies. At naptimes, I'd lie between two children, rubbing their backs and singing, until they fell asleep. Then, to meet a very personal need, I'd pick up a book lying on the bedside table and read for one hour before tackling housework again.

Lining up priorities with enduring values opened a new window for me. New life entered. The trapped feeling went away. In its place came cherished memories.

David's Discovery

God's order comes to us in the haphazard.[29]

One late afternoon, I was standing by the kitchen sink, peeling potatoes for supper. My husband and children would soon be coming home from school. I wanted supper and dishes out of the way so I could go over my notes for a talk that I would be giving to a group of young mothers in the evening.

I was going to speak on making memories. "In our frantic schedules, let's slow down a bit," I would encourage us mothers. "Let's not forget doing fun-filled activities with our children, like collecting leaves on a nature hike, or spending an evening doing crafts, or baking cookies together."

Just then my young son burst through the kitchen door. "Mom, come see what I found," he called out, excitedly. On his way home from school, David had seen something important that he wanted to share with me. But what a time to do it! I glanced at the kitchen clock on the wall. I hadn't scheduled a trip to the park before supper. I needed to move right along if I was going to be ready for the meeting. It would have to wait.

"Come on, Mom!" The urgency in my son's voice and the eager look on his face told me it couldn't wait. Chafing inwardly at the interrupted routine but feeling that I owed it to him, I dropped the potato peeler and followed my son outside.

At an old hollow tree, David pointed up. "Look inside, Mom. Aren't they cute?"

I peered inside. In a neat little nest, three scrawny, feather-less robins squeaked helplessly. With open beaks on long spindly necks, they scanned the air for food. Their bulging eyes were still covered, and bits of blue eggshell clung to their fuzzy bodies. *Amazing*, I thought, *I've never seen the miracle of a robin's birth up close before.*

As I returned home, I knew there would be one more thing I would tell the women that night: "Above all, let's heed the excited call of our children, 'Mom, Dad, see what I found.' If we don't, we might run right past what could be the most memorable event of the day."

I know, for most of what I saw and did on that day, so many years ago, I have forgotten. But the unplanned trip to the park with David remains a shining memory.

I Needed to Listen[30]

In a household of seven people, crowding one week's cleaning into one short day can be overwhelming, especially if you have the sudden urge to be absolutely thorough!

Last week, I decided I had put up with superficial, makeshift cleaning for too long. Everywhere I looked in our ten-room home, a mess stared me in the face.

I could have sworn that the children hadn't looked under their beds for a year. The interior of the refrigerator was splattered with melted butter hardened into waxy blobs (from the time the children made popcorn), while the oven was caked with gooey lumps of charcoal from the last time I baked apple pies. The big hall closet was overflowing with bags of unmatched socks (our lost and found department), and the floor of every closet in every bedroom seemed heaped with clothes that should have been on hangers. Jonathan, our four-year-old, had emptied his huge toy box in search of a piece of Tupperware animal. It was the perfect sort of mid-autumn day to clean windows before the early frosts!

Usually, I dive right in and keep going all day at top speed. I don't even take time to eat or to sit for five minutes and read the mail. I resent it if the phone rings. Hurriedly, I sneak glances at Jonathan and instruct him to "play nicely."

Before long, there's a tightness in my throat—then a painful squeezing around my heart. I can feel my pulse throbbing in my wrists and an ominous weight pushing against the top of my head. By nightfall, I am so wound up that I toss and turn and sleep fitfully, or not at all.

Well, this day also I plunged ahead, determined to make an end of all this mess. As the morning progressed, I felt a strange tugging towards the bedroom, like the tugging of a child who wants to tell me something.

"Dear Lord," I said, "I'd love to come and sit quietly in Your presence for a few minutes, but this morning I just can't. I've got too much to do. I'm sure You understand."

The tugging persisted.

"I'll finish what I'm doing and then I'll come," I promised.

The tugging became stronger.

Finally, I consented and went into the bedroom. I knelt down and said, "Well, here I am, Lord. What is it You want to tell me?" My Bible fell open to the following words: "The LORD your God is with you, he is mighty to save. He will take great delight in you, he will quiet you with his love, he will rejoice over you with singing."[31] I closed my eyes and whispered, "Almighty God delights in me! Wow!' I could hardly comprehend such love. I read the words over and over, basking in His pleasure.

Full of joy and marveling at His presence, I went back to work.

In the afternoon, still up to my eyeballs in jobs to be done, the tugging returned. "But, Lord," I said, "I already know that You love me and that You are with me. What more is there today?"

Come and see, He seemed to be saying.

Again, I reluctantly went to the bedroom

Read Jonathan a story, the Voice said.

That completed, He instructed, *Now snuggle in beside him, and close your eyes.*

Soon, I was sound asleep. An hour later, I awoke. Refreshed, I returned to my work.

When my husband came home that evening, he remarked, "This house has really seen a transformation. Even the windows sparkle! You must have worked awfully hard today."

I smiled. It wasn't until a few days later that I shared with him what really happened.

My Son's Accident

I could hear my son's screams the moment I got off the elevator. Quickly, I entered the pediatric unit littered with toys. Two white-clad nurses scurried towards a room on the far left. I raced after them. Jonathan's small body was almost swallowed up in an adult bed. A steel pin, like giant pincers, bit into his bruised and swollen elbow. A steel bar above the bed, with a rope and pulley suspending heavy weights, kept his left arm elevated at right angles. Jonathan's small body thrashed up and down. "I want to get up," he screamed. "I want to get out."

He can't even sit up or roll over, let alone get out of bed, I shuddered.

"Let me near him, please," I whispered to the nurse.

I pushed my right hand underneath my son's thrashing body and leaned over to hug him. "Cry all you want," I said.

Then I buried my hot face into his blue hospital gown, too heartsick to cry. We had been so sure God was answering our prayers for a speedy recovery. But two attempts at setting the broken elbow had failed. After four hours in surgery, the bone specialist had spoken with us in the waiting room. "The bones won't stay in place. Too many torn muscles. Pinning the elbow was the only option."

"How long in hospital?" my husband had asked.

"One month—at least."

One month! Like this? I shuddered. Our active nine year old couldn't even sit still for five minutes. I had affection-ately called him our family's exclamation mark, for whatever the other four did, he did with even more energy. That is what sometimes got him into trouble, like this accident.

Jonathan and his sister Cathy had been racing across the yard, jumping over piles of golden maple leaves I'd raked earlier in the day. Suddenly, my son had slipped and crashed to the ground. Their screams had sent me running from the kitchen. Seeing his elbow jammed into his upper arm and his hand twisted up toward his shoulder, I knew it was bad.

Before surgery, I had asked some of our friends to pray that things would go well, but now, listening to my son's cries, I thought, *Nothing's going well. Everything is taking its natural course just as though we had never prayed.*

"Get me out of this bed, please, Mom," he whimpered.

"I can't do that, Jonathan," I said, "But I'll ask the nurse if I can stay for the night. Then tomorrow, I'll get your favourite books and some toys and treats."

During the long night, I dozed in a chair beside my son's bed. When I heard his soft moaning, I took his good hand and gave it three squeezes. "I—love—you," I said with each squeeze. I felt so helpless. How I wished I could take his pain away, but all I could do was sit here and squeeze his hand.

The following day, Jonathan's whole family trooped into the pediatric unit with arms full of his favourite things. Soon, a monkey hung from the horizontal steel bar above his bed. His threadbare teddy lay beside him with one paw bandaged up and suspended in traction. A stack of comic books lay on the bedside table, on top of storybooks. His father brought him a giant Slurpee, two chocolate bars, and potato chips.

As Jonathan devoured his treats and listened to the banter of his siblings, a weak smile flitted across his face. But as we prepared to go home, he begged, "Take me home now."

I leaned over and whispered, "Jesus is staying with you, and don't forget, we'll be back tomorrow."

"Okay," he grunted.

The following day, as I entered our son's room, I found him with a lap desk across his chest. He was reading a comic book.

"I got to watch TV today," he grinned.

Since there was no television in his room, I wondered out loud, "How did you do that?"

"The nurses shoved my bed into the play area."

"The whole bed through that narrow door?"

"Yeah!" he grinned.

He's not as down today, I sighed with relief. *The twinkle in his eyes is back.*

Soon, his days had a pattern: after hospital routine, school lessons in the morning (the school board had provided a private tutor); in the afternoon, television programs; in the evening, company.

One day, Jonathan showed me a sheaf of papers the teacher had brought him: Get well letters from each of his classmates! We laughed at the funny illustrations done in pencil crayons.

One little boy had felt so sorry for his bedridden friend that he had emptied his piggy bank and sent a special treat to Jonathan.

By Halloween, our son had been flat on his back for several weeks. To mark the holiday, his sisters dressed as Bozo the clown and Pippy Longstocking, and his father dressed in crazily mismatched clothes. Jonathan giggled with delight.

One day in early December, after another series of X-rays, the specialist announced the bone had fused well enough for the traction to be removed. We would be able to take our son home in time for Christmas.

Of course that was not the end of Jonathan's ordeal. Even though the traction was removed, he couldn't straighten his arm. His elbow seemed stuck at right angles. For three months, our son exercised, with me cheering him on. Finally his arm straightened, but he could not flex it beyond the ninety-degree angle.

Seeking an explanation, we consulted our family doctor. Seeing the deformity, he shook his head. "The arm will have to be rebroken," he said glumly. "The bones have fused in the wrong position."

Jonathan lowered his eyes, trying hard to keep his top lip from quivering.

Fear raged through my body. *No! God, not that again!*

"Before we do anything," the doctor continued, "I'd like you to see a bone specialist in Vancouver. Take along these X-rays."

What a relief to hear the renowned specialist say, "Since your son's arm is still growing, I'm quite sure this will correct itself. In my opinion, no further surgery is required at this time."

To celebrate this good news, I bought Kentucky Fried Chicken, and my son and I picnicked in Vancouver's famous Queen Elizabeth Park. Jonathan kept doing lopsided cartwheels on the grass, and I couldn't stop smiling.

The specialist's prognosis was accurate. Through the years, Jonathan's arm became almost completely normal. He still can't touch his shoulder, but that has not hampered him in any way. Throughout high school, he has played every sport, including football. He engaged in heavy manual work on weekends and summer holidays to put himself through university. Today, he's a doctor of medicine.

"Do you think your long hospital stay influenced your career choice?" I asked him recently.

"Probably," he grinned.

A scene flashed through my mind. A boy pinned to a bed

screaming, "Let me out of here." At the time, I'd chafed at the cruelty of my son's suffering. Now, glimpsing a tiny bit of a bigger plan, I marvel that something that seemed so wrong could end up being right after all.

Jonathan's Passport[32]

I can carry my own," my son Jonathan said, reaching across the airplane seat for his passport.

"No, I'll hold onto it," I said, putting it into my own pocket. "It's an important document, and I'm—"

"Afraid I'm gonna lose it. Mom, I'm *sixteen*."

In fact, he'd turned sixteen that very day. We were on our way to Switzerland, just the two of us, taking a much-needed holiday together. It had been a difficult year—full of family illness and hardship—and I felt that Jonathan deserved to get away on a trip like this.

Back home, friends had warned me to be very careful with our documents. Some of their friends had recently been robbed on a trip abroad, and I was determined it would not happen to us. An unsuspecting person like Jonathan had to be protected; that's why it was up to me to carry our valuables. Jonathan thought it was silly the way I fastened them in a pocket of my slacks with three strong safety pins.

When we arrived in the beautiful old city of Basel, the first thing we did was buy Swiss travel passes for travelling by bus and train during the day and staying in youth hostels at night. Soon we boarded our first train and were rolling past quaint chalets with trailing red roses and colourful window boxes. Steep vineyards graced the shores of pristine lakes; glistening waterfalls cascaded from rocks overhead.

After the conductor came through to check our travel passes, I automatically reached for Jonathan's.

"I'm keeping this," he said firmly, then asked again for his passport.

"No," I insisted, "That's safer in my pocket." Then I added, "I'm just being careful."

"Yeah, you don't think I can be careful," Jonathan said, turning away to look out the window. I glanced at him now, so handsome in his black windbreaker with his school mascot stamped on it. He'd just have to understand that I meant well.

The days went by, and one morning we took a mountain railway and inched up a steep Alpine incline to a small town called Kleine Scheidegg. Sparkling in the sunlight, the snow-capped glaciers of the Eiger, the Moench, and the Jungfrau towered over us as we sat on a knoll and ate our picnic lunch.

"Let's go higher," Jonathan said, pointing to a small footpath that wriggled into the undulating mountainside. He started off excitedly, and at a flat rock I caught up with his long strides.

Out of breath and tired, I said, "I'll stay here while you go on." Sitting down on the rock, I watched my son climb another knoll, and then I lost sight of him.

A rumbling noise made me look up. I hadn't noticed the darkening clouds, nor the quickening breeze. Soon big drops of rain splashed on my face. *Why isn't Jonathan coming back?* I stared into the menacing clouds that enveloped the mountain where I'd seen him last. Fear clutched at my heart.

As the rain beat down in sheets, I had no choice but to find shelter. Hoping Jonathan would realize where I'd gone, I hurried back down the path to the little train station and huddled on a bench. As the minutes ticked by, I kept staring at the door. Why wasn't he coming? What had happened to him? I was wild with worry and guilt. Why had I let him go off by himself? *Dear God*, I prayed, *watch over Jonathan. Bring him back safely.*

Thirty minutes later, Jonathan appeared, half running, half sliding down the path, his wet hair dripping water down his flushed cheeks, his windbreaker and shorts clinging to his soaked body.

"Jonathan!" I cried. "Thank goodness you're safe! How did you know what to do?"

"The choices weren't all that great," he said, his mouth curving slightly in the way it does when I've asked a dumb question.

Fearful as I'd been for him, now I replaced fear with pride. He'd certainly conducted himself well in this crisis. Moreover, I recalled how he'd often understood the train and bus timetables much better than I had. Now I studied this tall, good-looking son beside me and thought, *Maybe I should trust him with a little more independence.*

All too soon the time came for us to say goodbye to Switzerland. During our last night in that picture-book country, I unpinned my pocket and took out its contents. My Swiss travel pass, and all but two traveller's cheques were used up. Our youth hostel booklet had collected interesting stamps of the places where we'd slept. Only one stamp in our passports so far, but we'd collect two more: one in Germany and the other in Seattle when we arrived there day after tomorrow.

As I put the items back into my pocket, I fumbled with the safety pins. The bulge over my left flank did look rather ridiculous. I could almost hear Jonathan once more ridiculing my overzealous precaution.

Impulsively, I dropped the bag into my purse, pulled my wallet from my suitcase, and sank it into my purse as well. *He's right*, I said to myself. *I'm altogether too fearful.*

And so Jonathan and I took a train to Frankfurt, where we'd board a plane for Seattle the next morning. In the Frankfurt station, we decided there was no need to lug our heavy baggage to the youth hostel, so we carried it to the check-in counter. My purse hung securely over my shoulder. I squatted to open the suitcase to take out a nightie and housecoat, things I would use for our last night in Europe.

Suddenly, a strange feeling came over me. *What's wrong?* I thought. *Why do I feel so strange? Oh, I know. I feel—lighter. My left shoulder feels lighter.*

The moment I realized my purse was gone, panic made me gasp for breath. I could hardly speak, but I managed to stammer, "I've been robbed, Jonathan."

"My passport, too?"

"Yes."

His face blanched and he turned away.

My own fear threatened to overwhelm me: here we were in a foreign country, without legal papers, no plane tickets to get home, not a piece of identification to prove who we were, and no money or charge card to pay for lodging and food. I didn't even have enough money for a phone call or the public washroom.

Leaving Jonathan with the luggage, I raced around the huge train station in search of the police office. There I reported the theft.

When the officer heard I had a son in the train station, he asked me to get him. Wide-eyed, I listened as Jonathan gave a detailed description of a man wearing a flowered shirt who had thrust a handful of coins toward him and chattered in a foreign language. Also, he described a small dark man who'd flitted past us. Two officers took note of his intelligent observations. Then we were left on our own.

A kind stranger had overheard our conversation with the officers and gave us money, enough for a day's food and lodging. Early the following morning we headed out to the airport. I figured the authorities at the airport would need a little extra time to check out the details of our citizenship and flight. Even though we had no passports and tickets, I felt hopeful that in this high-tech age, all the necessary information would be in a computer file somewhere.

But at the Pan Am ticket counter, we were told, "Nobody travels without a passport and a ticket." We'd have to go to Bonn to have interim passports made. We'd have to buy two replacement tickets from Frankfurt to Seattle—and wait for a flight with two available seats. It might take up to two weeks.

Stunned, I asked to speak with a supervisor. He shook his head at the gravity of our situation but agreed to make some phone calls in an attempt to get us onto our scheduled flight. "Have you at least one piece of ID, madam?" he asked me. I shook my head no.

"I've got some," Jonathan said brightly and then produced his school identification card and his Swiss travel pass.

I hung my head. If I hadn't been so obstinate, Jonathan would now be able to show his passport, and our chances of going home on that flight might have improved. I'd prided myself on being able to look after both of us. And now? Was God trying to show me something?

I thought back to the thunderstorm up at Kleine Scheidegg when I'd felt so small and scared and helpless. I'd asked God to watch over Jonathan, and Jonathan had come running down the mountain safely. I'd trusted God, but how little trust I'd placed in this bright young son of mine. Perhaps it was time to let go and trust him more.

A kind couple took us to the Canadian embassy in Bonn, where we obtained emergency passports, and we flew home just two days after the robbery. When we boarded the plane this time, Jonathan had his passport and ticket in his own pocket. After all, he'd demonstrated that he already had his passport to maturity.

Tattooed Angel[33]

One glorious spring day, my two teens and I headed up Mount Baker for a picnic. At the snow line, we sat down. The sun warmed our backs; the towering peaks of other Cascade mountains gleamed before us; trickles of melted snow gurgled beside us as we ate our lunch of Kentucky Fried Chicken, fries, and coleslaw.

All too soon, it was time to go home. Cathy hopped into the passenger seat; Jonathan got into the back seat; and I slid behind the steering wheel and turned the ignition key. The car gave a sickening moan. Again, I tried to start the car, with the same result. Each time I turned the key, the moan grew softer until it died away altogether.

"We'll flag down a car and ask them to jumper cable us," I said, opening the trunk where such equipment was kept. Wouldn't you know it? No jumper cables.

"Never mind. Somebody will be able to help us out." I tried to sound cheerful.

Stationing myself beside the road, I flagged down the few cars that passed by. Nobody had jumper cables. Nobody offered to help. We left the hood open and sat down beside the car and waited.

A pickup rumbled down the mountain. As it barrelled past us, I got a glimpse of a big sign on the front fender. "Sad Sack," it said. *That's what we must look like about now, a bunch of sad sacks,* I thought.

A gravelly roar made me look up. "Sad Sack" was

coming back. A young man with brawny arms covered in large tattoos leaned out the window.

One look at those arms and I knew he wouldn't help us either. He wasn't the type. But he surprised me by asking, "Having troubles?"

"Yes, but I don't have jumper cables."

"No problem. He'll know what to do," his companion beamed. "He's a good mechanic, the best in the county."

As he worked on our car, taking off one part and sticking his thumb in another, my eyes got wider and wider. At different intervals, I hopped behind the wheel and turned on the ignition. Finally it caught, and a healthy roar filled the car.

We thanked "Sad Sack" warmly, but he wasn't finished yet. "We'll follow you down," he said, "just in case."

Each time I glanced into our rear view mirror and saw the reassuring pickup behind us, I felt comforted—and a bit chagrined. How wrong my short-sighted judgment had been. *From now on I want to see people as God sees them*, I thought, *with the heart.*

Lisa's Chicken[34]

Late one night, it was chicken-catching time at the neighbour's barn. In the darkness of night, giant hands grabbed unsuspecting sleeping hens and stuffed them into cages to be shipped to the butchery. One chicken, unwilling to accept that her end had come, made a dash for the door and escaped. She flapped her way across a wide pasture beset with teasing dogs and ended up in our backyard. The following morning we found her, almost denuded of feathers, lying on her side, eyes closed, gasping for breath. I wanted to put her out of her misery, but Lisa, our compassionate teen, objected. "Mom, after all she's been through, we can't kill her," she said. Gently she lifted the almost-dead hen into her arms and hugged her. Lovingly she nursed her back to health and strength.

In time, Gertrude Esmeralda—as my daughter named her pet—grew lovely white feathers. She wore her bright red comb like a crown. With confidence, she roamed across the entire yard, pecking here and there. She would strut up to the dog's dish and peck at his food while he sat at a safe distance waiting for his turn. At times she would fly up onto the lean-to at our kitchen window, peer in with sprightly eyes, and loudly cackle her joy at having laid an egg. Other times she would scratch the windowpane, reminding me it was time for another handful of popcorn. She knew she belonged.

Our chicken is absolutely confident that the people who cared enough to save her will also give her everything else she needs to live a full life, I mused. *She has more faith in me than I have in God.*

The absurdity brought a chuckle. A warm realization washed over me that the God who saved me will also give me everything I need to live a full and abundant life. For He had promised, "And my God will meet all your needs according to his glorious riches in Christ Jesus."[35] But to make them mine, I had to come boldly and help myself to His abundance.

I had to begin acting like a member of God's household.

Watch Over My Son[36]

When my son Jonathan announced that he and two buddies from high school would be driving to Disneyland in California—over 3,000 kilometres from our home in southern British Columbia—I panicked. Jonathan, at seventeen, had driven barely one year, and the other two boys, being younger, didn't drive at all. Remembering the traffic on the freeways in California, I worried, "What if your old Micra Nissan breaks down on the freeway? What if you get lost and you end up in the wrong part of Los Angeles? What if you have an accident?"

Jonathan waved all my worries aside. "Don't worry, Mom. We'll be all right."

"Your aunt and uncle in Oregon would love to see you," I said. "Why don't you visit them?" Translated: *It's not nearly as far, and besides, I can phone you to see that you're all right.*

"We might stop there," Jonathan said. "Before we head south."

"I don't want you to go south," I said more firmly. "It's not a good idea."

The following morning, we hugged. He squeezed his six-foot-four body behind the steering wheel and flashed me a big grin. "See you in a week," he said. The gleam in his eyes told me how much he was looking forward to his first real flight into independence.

As I watched the tail lights disappear down the road, I tried to conjure up excitement for him. After all, he deserved one last fling before another heavy school year began.

In the evening, I phoned my sister. Yes, the boys had arrived safely. They'd be staying overnight, and in the morning they'd be heading south.

My son was determined to go to Los Angeles. Should I talk to him once more to try to stop him? I decided against it. After all, before he had left in the morning, we had read together Psalm 121: "Remember, the Lord will watch over your coming and going." Now I had better demonstrate that I really believed the words. Still, I couldn't shake a feeling of uneasiness.

On the afternoon of the third day, a man from Los Angeles phoned. "I don't want to alarm you," he said slowly, "but your son rear-ended my car."

My heart skipped a beat. I couldn't utter a sound.

"Are you still there?"

"Yes," I whispered.

"The boys are all right," he quickly added. "But your son's car is pretty banged up."

"Where is he?" I asked. "Can you put me in touch with him?"

Unfortunately, he didn't know the name or phone number of the garage where he'd last seen the boys. As I hung the receiver back in its cradle, I slumped to a chair. *Great! A banged-up car and no money for repairs.* All day I wanted the telephone to ring. I wanted my son to be on the other end. I wanted to assure him that things would work out. I wanted to wire him some money. But Jonathan didn't phone that day, nor the next, nor the next.

What do you do when worry for your son and his friends threatens to overwhelm you? You cling to a promise from God. I kept repeating Psalm 121 over and over again, personalizing the words: "He who watches over you [the boys]...will neither slumber nor sleep. The Lord will watch over your [the boys'] coming and going." You cling to a memory of God's faithfulness in the past. When I had been robbed of my purse, losing our tickets for home, our passports, and all our money, God had worked in such wondrous ways that my son and I had come home just two days behind schedule. And you try to keep busy. I engaged in mind-absorbing activities, such as reading a book and writing an article. I humoured myself saying, "It's not time to worry yet. Give yourself another day or two, and then you can worry all you like."

Also, I asked others to pray. Throughout the year, I had met with other mothers to pray for our children on a regular basis. Now I dialed up some of the women and asked them to pray specifically for safety for the boys.

One day, a week later, near midnight, Jonathan sauntered through the back door into our kitchen, oblivious to the worry he'd caused me. His eyes registered shock when he discovered I already knew about the accident. He said he'd wanted to tell me in person, thus sparing me unnecessary worry. "I was plenty worried myself," he said. "But you know what, Mom? My banged-up car purred all the way home. Amazing." Then he flashed me a big grin, "You must have been praying."

I smiled. My son had gained much more than a taste of independence. He'd seen first-hand how God takes care of His children. And to think God did it without me!

Esther's Rose

E sther, our vivacious teen, burst into the kitchen after school one day mid-February and, waving something at me, she sang out, "I got a rose!"
"That's nice," I said absent-mindedly.

As head of a refugee sponsorship program for our church, I was preoccupied with the problems that needed to be solved before our refugee family arrived in a few days: Find appropriate housing, complete with furniture and appliances. Stock the shelves with groceries. Arrange for daily transportation to and from school, the doctor, and church. Since the refugees wouldn't be speaking English, I had to arrange for time in my busy schedule to take them shopping and to introduce them to unfamiliar ways in their new country.

Scarcely aware of Esther's dashing around the house, I mulled over recent setbacks. The person who'd agreed to pick up our refugee family at the airport wasn't able to make it, and I'd have to find someone else. But who?

"Bye, Mom," my daughter yelled, as she slammed through the back door. "I'll be back at eleven."

I watched her little green car shoot out of the driveway on its way to her after-school job at McDonald's. Suddenly, my mind snapped to attention. What was it she'd been so excited about?

Why, Valentine's Day! What was it she had said? A rose? I hurried into her bedroom and picked up a small vase that cradled a perfect red rose bud. My gregarious daughter had received her very first rose from an admirer. What a special time in a girl's life! She'd wanted to share her precious moment with me, and I had let worries steal an intimate moment from us.

As I held the flower of her teenage romance, I remembered the excitement I had felt at my daughter's birth, the thrill of tracing her growth, and the joy of seeing her develop her many talents. Why hadn't I been more alert to this new phase in her life? Still, all was not lost. When she came home, I would ask her to tell me about the rose.

She's Leaving Home[38]

My daughter Cathy stands poised in the middle of her old bedroom, directing her new husband. "Eric, that box can go now."

My new son-in-law easily lifts a box of wedding gifts and carries it outside. As I watch him shove it into the back of their van, I feel a twinge of sudden fear. Each time my daughter has left home before, she left with a gym bag and a backpack. Now there are boxes. *This is permanent,* I realize.

As Cathy lifts an oil painting of Mount Baker off a wall and slides it into a large cardboard box, I want to protest: *You can't take that! The wall looks so empty without it.* I remember how thrilled we both were when my daughter's painting was chosen for an art display in her high school. But I bite my tongue and say nothing.

Next, her pencil drawing of a ballerina descends into a waiting box, joined by the figurines Cathy collected throughout childhood...

I'm jarred as each reminder of her life at home is packed and carted away.

Before me stands a woman eager to establish her own home. And I'm afraid, knowing the hardships that await these two people, so young and vulnerable, as they plunge into married life together.

How is it possible? I wonder. *Where has the time gone?* On a bright September morning just sixteen short years ago I walked with Cathy, her small hand in mine, to South Poplar school.

She wouldn't stay alone a half hour in Sunday school; how would she survive a half day in kindergarten?

"No problem, Mrs. Lescheid," her teacher soothed. "Cathy will be just fine."

During grade one, I walked with her past farmhouses skirting neatly groomed raspberry fields to a friend's house halfway between our home and school. For the first few weeks, she hid behind me as I knocked on the door, but one day she pushed ahead of me. I noticed that when my friend addressed her at the door, she lifted her little face so they could have eye contact. I gave my daughter's shoulder a squeeze. *She's becoming braver!* I rejoiced.

When Cathy was nine, she had a part in the school play *The Gingerbread Boy.* Typically, Cathy said little about her role. *She's probably in the back row of a choral group,* I thought. *It will take all the courage she has just to be onstage.*

On the night of the performance, the lights dimmed, and Mr. Gingerbread walked on stage and plopped into an easy chair. Mrs. Gingerbread entered, wearing the white bibbed apron I had made and decorated with ruffled eyelet lace. I blinked. *My Cathy? Taking a lead role?* My heart pounded. She looked so small, so fragile. And yet, with head held high, my daughter sang a beautiful solo.

I wondered what magic her teachers had used to get my shy little girl to perform such a brave feat. And then I remembered the ring of confidence in her kindergarten teacher's voice as she'd said on that first day of school, "Cathy will be just fine!"

Do my words convey that same confidence at home? I wondered. *Or does my anxiety about her tinge all of our conversations with fear?*

More than anything, I wanted Cathy to have self-confidence. I remembered my own struggle with low self-esteem and how my faith in God and some well-timed words of encouragement had helped me believe in myself. So I determined that I would pass on words of faith, not fear, to Cathy. To make them more tangible, I'd scribble my words of encouragement on pieces of scrap paper and leave them on her bed or on her desk.

Cathy continued to amaze me with her achievements. But sometimes her fragile self-esteem suffered a cruel blow. During those times, I'd hold her trembling body and pray she'd learn to overcome her doubts. With persistence, hope, and prayers, we survived her teenage years.

Shortly after Cathy entered university, she introduced her dad and me to Eric. "Just a friend," my daughter assured me.

About a year later, during a break from school, Cathy and I strolled through a park. As I peppered her with questions about her life at school, she answered in monosyllables. I wondered what was bothering her.

Just as we reached the car, she blurted, "Eric and I want to get married."

Worrisome, fearful thoughts rushed forward, and I wanted to say, "You're too young! You've just begun your studies. How will you support yourselves?"

Instead, an echo in my heart like a clear ringing bell stopped me: *Speak faith, not fear.*

I took a deep breath. "You know best," I said quietly. "I trust your judgment, Cathy."

She whirled around and exploded, "I thought you'd be mad."

"No, I'm not mad," I said, hoping that my misgivings didn't show. Then I added, "What kind of a wedding do you want? Can we talk about it?"

A simple wedding, elegant in style. What's more, she wanted me to take part in the preparations. I sewed bridesmaid dresses in emerald green and folded invitations made on the computer. We scouted around for a reasonable catering service and decorated the church hall. On the wedding day, I snapped photos of the bride under apple trees in our backyard. Seeing her dressed in a plain but elegant gown and clutching a basket of wild flowers, with her long brown hair rippling in the breeze, I felt my pulse quicken. Was there ever a more beautiful bride?

My daughter pauses in her packing. She picks up a large scrapbook and begins to turn the pages.

"Neat!" she exclaims. "I'd forgotten I had this."

I step closer and peer over her shoulder. On the pages are bits of memorabilia from her life at home: birthday parties, photos and notes from friends, ribbons won in soccer, a newspaper clipping of her as the old woman in *The Gingerbread Boy,* a note from her drama teacher congratulating her on her performance in *Anne of Green Gables.*

But what I notice most are the bits of scrap paper with *my* handwriting: "Thanks, Cathy, for cleaning your room," "Thanks for being faithful to your piano practices and for telling your baby brother stories," "I'm so proud of you! You were an excellent Marilla," "Welcome home, Cath! Imagine winning a silver in the Pacific Basin Choir Festival in Honolulu."

When I wrote those words of commendation so long ago, I had no idea how much my daughter would cherish them. Now as I see her pack the scrapbook, my heart feels light and warm.

"What a pack rat I am," she laughs, as she shuts the book. "I don't throw anything away."

"I'm glad," I whisper.

Gems of Truth: Wise Words

"The words of the wise are like prodding goads, and firmly fixed [in the mind] like nails."[39]

Some years ago, in Yugoslavia, an altar boy dropped a chalice of wine. The priest shouted at the boy, "You clumsy good-for-nothing. Get out of my sight." Humiliated and discouraged, the altar boy fled from the church and never entered it again. Many years later, he became a powerful communist leader. President Tito was his name.

An altar boy in America dropped a chalice of wine also. As it lay shattered on the floor, the boy was mortified. The priest turned to the boy and said, "Never mind. One day, you'll be in my position." The boy's strained face relaxed. He resolved to be more careful in the future. Years later, this boy became a prominent American Roman Catholic clergyman and titular archbishop of Newport, England. His name? Fulton John Sheen.

What made the difference? A few words and how they were spoken. Our words have a powerful influence to imprison or to inspire, to act like goads prodding people on in different directions. Today, let us speak words of faith and encouragement, not fear and condemnation.

Prayer: Father, may the words of my mouth bring pleasure to You and bring encouragement and hope to all whom I come in contact with today.

Letting Go

Lisa was our free spirit. She'd do cartwheels on the front lawn—in the nude—then hide behind a bush when she heard a car approaching. She bubbled with life and fun and laughter. She played high-school basketball, was active in her church's youth group, and worked hard at her studies in the accelerated academic program. I figured she was a happy, well-adjusted teenager, perhaps a bit too serious about changing the world, but then it didn't hurt to have a worthy goal. Besides, she seemed to be enjoying life. Upon graduation from high school, she received a scholarship and, at age seventeen, entered university. Of our five children, Lisa, the middle one, demanded the least of my attention and gave me the fewest worries.

After a year, my daughter quit university and joined a mission. Four years later she quit the mission, but she was not ready to settle down. I sensed a deep unhappiness and restlessness in her, which sent her on a search across the world. She studied Mandarin in China; she taught school in Swaziland; she hitchhiked across South Africa. Many times I didn't know where she was or what she was doing or if she were still alive.

At home in Canada, she worked at all kinds of odd jobs: in kitchens, recycling plants, and other short-term jobs. She drove an old jalopy, which became her home.

How I blamed myself for my daughter's unhappiness! I felt I had neglected her. I should have spent more time with her. I should have paid more attention to what she was saying. I should have seen it coming. You know how we mothers beat ourselves up with *I should have!*

During those ten difficult years, the only things that provided some comfort for me were prayer and God's word. Repeatedly I would take my daughter to God. "Dear Lord, You know where Lisa is right now. You watch over her coming and her going," I'd pray. "You know what she is doing, for You never slumber nor sleep. Place Your hand upon her now, and keep her from all harm." Again I'd pray: "Lord Jesus, You are the good Shepherd and take good care of Your sheep. Go in search of Lisa now, and bring her home safely."

One day when my failures loomed large, I grabbed my Bible and began reading, "But you know that he [Christ] appeared so that he might take away our sins."[40] The words seemed to be lit up with neon lights. God was saying to me, "Yes, you are guilty of imperfect mothering. But never mind, for this reason Jesus came into the world: to die for your sin. You are forgiven. Now, you must forgive yourself and trust Me to use even your mistakes for good in your daughter's life."

Gradually I began to see that I was not responsible for my daughter's unhappiness. I needed to let go of my expectations of her and of myself. At this difficult time, a friend gave me a poem which helped me understand the letting go process.

To "let go" does not mean to stop caring; it means I can't do it for someone else.

To "let go" is not to enable but to allow learning from natural consequences.

To "let go" is to admit powerlessness, which means the outcome is not in my hands.

To "let go" is not to fix but to be supportive.

To "let go" is not to judge but to allow another to be a human being.

To "let go" is not to be in the middle arranging all the outcomes but to allow others to affect their own destinies.

To "let go" is not to be protective; it's to permit another to face reality.

To "let go" is not to deny but to accept.

To "let go" is not to nag, scold, or argue but instead to search out my own shortcomings and correct them.

To "let go" is not to adjust everything to my desires but to take each day as it comes and cherish myself in it.

To "let go" is not to regret the past but to grow and live for the future.

To "let go" is to fear less and to love more.

AUTHOR UNKNOWN

I discovered that when you love someone deeply, letting go is incredibly hard. Yet I must let go, for I do not own what I love. Repeatedly I've reminded myself that by releasing my grasp I'm allowing God to work in my daughter His beautiful design for her. He loves my daughter with an everlasting love, and He will take care of her much better than I ever could.

After ten tumultuous years, Lisa went back to university and completed her master's degree in biology. Because of all her travels, she's fluent in several languages. She's happily married and wonderfully connected with her family. Both Lisa and her husband have a passion for working with young people and for sharing their life experiences through writing and photography. Because of their wide travels and many talents, they're very well qualified.

God has done so much more than I asked Him for, and it happened because I got out of the way and let Him do it.

Children Are Like Daffodils

Through a technicality, my youngest son lost his academic scholarship. Reeling in confusion, he worried how he would complete university. Meanwhile, his older brother, working feverishly on his doctorate in biology, became severely ill and was laid up for awhile.

As a parent, I grieve when I see my children suffer like this. I feel they are too fragile to endure it. I want to protect them, to bail them out, to fix it for them. But even my best efforts cannot save them from life's hardships. Sometimes I wonder, *What is God doing in their lives?*

Spring temperatures in British Columbia's Fraser Valley (Canada), where I live, can be temperamental. Late in February last year, the warmth of the sun had tricked daffodils into forming swollen buds ready to burst into bloom. Then icy March winds raked across our garden. My daffodils lay like stiff pencils, frozen on the hard ground. *Ruined beyond repair,* I thought.

I snapped off a few flowers and carried them inside the house. How pathetic they looked! More ready for the trash can than the table. Dejectedly, I stuck them into a vase filled with warm water and placed them on the kitchen table.

The next morning, a golden surprise awaited me. My "wasted" flowers had become a bouquet of beautiful daffodils. As I studied each delicate bloom, I couldn't find a single blemish—not even a hint of yesterday's adversity. What overcoming power in a common daffodil!

If that is how God equips flowers, which are here today and gone tomorrow, how much more will He equip my children for life's adversities? I mused.

Yes, my children will get their share of suffering. I cannot prevent that. But when I see them slain by life's disappointments, sickness, and unfairness, I can offer open arms and a listening ear. I can nurture them with the warm water of my prayers. Who knows what golden virtues God is developing in them?

Poplar Trees and Children[41]

To the west of our country property, separating our backyard from a field of neatly groomed raspberry bushes, stand five enormous poplar trees. My husband and I planted the saplings when our five children were small—one for each child. Now as I gaze at the sturdy trees reaching for the sky, I wonder where the time has gone.

The youngest of our children left home to get married two years ago.

Our children's global interests often take them far away from home, to continents like Africa, Europe, Asia, and Australia. Many times I do not hear from them for months at a time. I worry about their safety. I worry that my imperfect mothering has not prepared them adequately for life's pitfalls. Sometimes I'm perplexed at the decisions they've made or the direction in which their lives are going. I want to shield them from trouble, but I can't.

At times like this, to calm my distraught spirit, I read specific promises God has given me concerning my children. I've highlighted them in my Bible. For quick, easy access I've also grouped them together—three pages typed, single-spaced. Scriptures such as the following:

"All your sons [children] will be taught by the LORD, and great will be your children's peace."[42]

"My eyes will watch over them for their good, and I will bring them back to this land...I will give them a heart to know Me, that I am the LORD."[43]

"[Your children will be] like poplar trees by flowing streams."[44]

As I gaze at the sturdy poplars in our backyard, I reflect how little I had to do with their growth. Beyond initial nurturing, I simply committed them to the Master of trees. *Aren't your children worth more than these?* As He asks the question, I can almost see the gentle smile of my Father. And once more, my heart is at peace.

Prayer: Father, into Your gentle, capable hands I commit my children.

Family

Your love, O LORD, reaches to the heavens,
your faithfulness to the skies.
Your righteousness is like the mighty mountains,
your justice like the great deep.

PSALM 36:5-6

You are All Things To Me:
The Promise every new sunrise brings
The Prize at each day's end
The Light at the end of a darkened tunnel
The Shade from the overpowering heat
The Rock when all around me gives way
The soft Palm of a supporting hand when I fall.
You fill all life with yourself, O Lord.

ABBIE TEH

Hope Stronger than Hurt

By all appearances we were the ideal Christian family. My husband and I loved the Lord and served Him wholeheartedly. Believing that a family that prays together stays together, we had daily family altar and took our five children to church. We reserved Friday nights for family fun—playing table games, going to basketball games in which one of our children played or to a special community event. During summers, we canoed rivers, explored mountains, and tented beside a lake. As a family we liked being together, and I figured it would go on forever.

That's why what happened one September afternoon hit us with the force of a tsunami and left us reeling in confusion and fear. It was the first day of school, and my husband, a high school teacher, was late in coming home. *He's probably picking up something in town*," I thought.

When he did come home, I knew something was very wrong. Normally he'd come through the door with a wide grin and a noisy "Hi!" This day, though, he looked down at the floor as he mumbled "I've been to see a doctor."

"Acute depression," the doctor said.

By the end of the first week, Bill signed himself into a psych ward. He felt out of control and was afraid of what he might do to himself and his family. Soon he was moved to the university hospital, and, because he attempted suicide there, he was transferred to the provincial psychiatric hospital.

Except for a few brief stays at home, Bill spent most of the next eight years in hospitals. When nothing helped, the doctors kept changing the diagnosis from acute depression to chronic depression, to bipolar disorder, then to dementia.

Life became a trail of confusion and frustration and pain. With every new psychiatrist—and we had at least a dozen—there was a new treatment and new drugs to try. My hopes would go up. *This will help.* When I saw my husband get worse instead of better, hopes came crashing down. This roller coaster of raised and dashed hopes creates havoc in a family.

Mental illness has a devastating effect on a family. Someone you love and feel safe with becomes a totally different person—fearful, rejecting, and threatening. When I was told that my husband was planning to kill me, I didn't know what to do with the information. I hopped into my car, turned on the ignition, and drove down the freeway. I didn't care where I was going as long as it took me away from such madness.

Our children, desperately hurt and confused, asked, "Where is God in all of this? Why doesn't He answer our prayers?" I wondered myself. Many people were praying, and I was so sure that God would answer by healing my husband and our family. Instead, the marriage ended in divorce. Bill was moved to a group home for people with dementia. Some of our children became estranged from the family. Some left the faith.

It seemed like I was losing everything I valued: my marriage, my family, my home, my reputation, and my writing ministry. (As a divorcee, people won't listen to you any more, I was told.) One day, a wave of despair came over me. *I can't take this any more. I'm cracking up,* I thought.

What happened next is hard to describe. Clear as a bell I heard a voice saying—not out loud but deep in my heart—"*Do you still have Jesus?*"

"Yes," I whispered.

"Then you have a centre. You have a refuge. You will be all right."

The Bible was the only book that offered me comfort and hope. It helped me make some sense out of my situation. Other godly people—Joseph, David, Daniel—had gone through terrible times; why not me? Moreover, it showed me a way of coping. I would read verses like this: "Blessed are those who trust in the Lord, whose trust is the Lord. They shall be like a tree planted by water, sending out its roots by the stream. It shall not fear when heat comes, and its leaves shall stay green; in the year of drought it is not anxious, and it does not cease to bear fruit."[45] "Keep your roots deep into Jesus and the Bible, and you will have all the resources you need," these verses said to me. One day at a time. One step at a time. Depending on Jesus. That's how I got through those tumultuous years. He gave me hope stronger than my hurts.

What did I learn in the process? Healing and true happiness come when you surrender all your expectations to God, our good Shepherd.

Expectations of God: how He would answer our prayers—When healing didn't come to my husband despite much earnest prayer and aggressive spiritual warfare, my faith was severely tested. I didn't understand what was happening, but I never doubted God's love for me. God is sovereign, and His plans for us are good. Still, He does not force His plans on us. God has given each of us the privilege of making choices and the responsibility of living with the conse- quences of those choices. It's possible for us to sabotage God's plans for our lives by wrongful choices. I believe this was a very real factor in my husband not being healed.

Expectations of myself—For years I blamed myself, thinking, *I should be able to make my husband happy. I should be able to shield my children from pain. I should be able to fix this*. As women—especially as mothers—we have been trained to fix things, right? *If I work hard enough, pray more and give more, then things will work out*, I thought. When they didn't, I felt like a colossal failure. The guilt was overwhelming.

It took me a long time to realize I was taking responsibility that God never intended me to have. I had made my desire to have a happy family my all-consuming goal. But since there were other persons making choices, I could not control the outcome. I couldn't save this family single-handedly.

Expectations of my husband: thinking that he would always be there for me—That we'll be a ministry team serving the Lord together. I came to realize that this dream could not happen unless both of us wanted this. Moreover, my husband could not meet all my love needs. No husband can. Only God can be there for us at all times. Only God loves perfectly. Only God can meet all of our needs.

Expectations of my children: that they would understand and support me—The fact is, when hurt is so deep, it's difficult to be objective. Looking for a cause, it's easy to blame one another. To shout at one another, "And you don't even care!" To pull away from each other into isolation. Grieving the loss of a family takes time. Each person grieves in his or her own unique way.

After many painful years, I parcelled up all my expectations, my disappointments, and my failures and handed them to God. *Here, Lord, I give this burden to you now. It's too heavy for me to carry. You are my Shepherd, and you have said that I shall not want any good thing. You know that I'm wanting right now. I need encouragement, guidance, emotional stability. I look to you to supply my needs.*" I prayed this prayer again and again, and God did meet my need in surprising ways, often through people I least expected. Other times, He showed me what I had to do to improve the situation. Being totally dependent upon God is one of the hardest things we Christians have to do in life. We fear the helplessness of it. We want to be in control. Still, God cannot work unless we surrender to Him. His way is always to work through weakness.

Giving to God what wasn't in my power to change, I focused on what I could change: myself. The danger was to hang onto hurtful words, to let bitterness creep in, and to allow self-pity to overwhelm me. An extremely helpful exercise was writing in journals. Writing helped me to validate my feelings and to focus on real issues. It cleared the mental confusion, to be able to see more clearly what God wanted me to do.

By faith I kept affirming, "It is safe to trust God, for He has my best interests at heart." Now, years later, I can say with deep conviction that "The LORD is gracious and compassionate, slow to anger and rich in love. The LORD is good to all; he has compassion on all he has made."[46]

Through time and much prayer, healing has come to our family. We are growing as persons and in our faith. Once more we love being together in family gatherings or in travels. Although Bill is living in a group home, the children keep in contact by phone, e-mail and visits.

What seemed to be the end was really a new beginning of a deeper relationship with God. It has led to greater maturity and a more fruitful ministry. God is using this painful experience as I minister to broken persons through writing and speaking. My book *Treasures of Darkness* is being used in Canada, U.S.A., and Australia.

I read of a woman who during the recent tsunami disaster in southeast Asia was saved from certain drowning by clinging to a palm tree floating beside her. When life hits us with a tsunami, Jesus is there in the water with us. Clinging to Him, we are saved. He raises us up to new vistas. Knowing Him is the most valuable relationship in the world.

If you would like to order *Treasures of Darkness,*
write to: hopeingod@uniserve.com.

Flowers Bloom for Me

My mother's home in town was about four kilometres from our country home. I often visited her on an afternoon. At the end of my visit, we usually inspected her many flower beds. Impatiens, nasturtiums, roses, geraniums, and a host of other flowers bloomed in profusion.

I usually enjoyed this ritual, but on this afternoon I listened half-heartedly to my mother's cheerful chatter. My mind was on my desperately ill husband. Yet I didn't want my mother to see the anguish I felt. I didn't want to burden her. Besides, I feared a reprimand. Emotional talk unnerved my mother. In the past, she had lectured me, "We do not give in to self-pity."

As my gaze followed her small frame, darting in and out of rose bushes, I thought, *Mother, you had reason to feel sorry for yourself. Why didn't you?* After seven years of marriage, she'd lost her husband to the insanity of the Second World War. Life had pummelled her; people had disappointed her. Yet, she'd managed to keep a sweet spirit. Her consistently upbeat attitude both amazed and infuriated me. Didn't she ever feel weak?

Suddenly, my mother stopped her chatter. She gazed into my face and whispered, "How's Bill?"

"Not good," I whispered back.

Her sky-blue eyes became moist. "I'm sorry," she murmured.

For a few moments she stared into a rose bush as though searching for something to say. "When life became unbearable for me," she said quietly. "I planted flowers. They always bloomed for me."

When I left her house, I determined, come spring, I would plant more flowers. For that reason, as soon as the danger of frost is past, you'll find me at the plant nursery hauling home flats of bedding plants and pots of flowers of every description. Later, when my yard is ablaze with colour, I see in each radiant bloom a personal love message from God.

Yes, flowers bloom for me too.

The Light of His Presence[47]

I found my seat in the middle section of a small theatre and sat down. All about me, people—mostly couples with small children—buzzed excitedly. We were about to see a senior high school production of *Anne of Green Gables*, and many of our teens were playing a part in it.

Although my daughter Cathy played Marilla (a leading role), my excitement was muted. *If only her dad could be here to see her,* I kept thinking. *He'd be so proud of her.* But a serious depression kept him confined to a provincial psychiatric hospital. His illness had thrown our family into one crisis after another. As the months passed and no improvement came, I felt locked inside a dark tunnel. Decisions forced themselves upon me, but often I didn't know what to do.

The theatre darkened. The curtains on the stage parted. A beam of light coming from a control room behind me illuminated the stage. Soon the story of Anne, a spirited orphan girl whose impulsiveness often got her into serious trouble, unfolded before us. As each conflict ended in a neat, sometimes hilarious, resolution, I thought, *Lord, light up my life like that stage.* I felt if God would give me more light, I'd be better equipped to make wise decisions.

Halfway through the first scene, an usher came down the aisle, guiding two latecomers. In his right hand, he held a flashlight forming a small circle of light at their feet. Slowly he moved ahead to the appropriate row; then he shone the light onto two vacant seats. He waited patiently until the man and woman had sat down. Then he turned off the flashlight and walked quietly back to the entrance.

That's how I lead you! The thought was as clear as though God had spoken audibly. *As you read My written Word and obey it, you'll have enough light to know what step to take next, and then there'll be more light for the next step, and the next. Obey the directive you do have. Trust Me. I will see to it that you get safely to the right place.*

His reassuring words wrapped themselves around me like a warm blanket.

Then I thought of the man in the control room doing his thing—throwing switches, moving the light around. As a technician, he had no personal interest in those people on the stage. All he wanted was a professional performance.

Is God like that? A cosmic technician interested only in a perfect performance? No!

In the Bible I read, "I will lead the blind by ways they have not known, along unfamiliar paths I will guide them; I will turn the darkness into light before them and make the rough places smooth. These are the things I will do; I will not forsake them."[48]

Of course, God, who cares deeply for His children, would want to be involved in the journey. He would choose the personal approach! Our Lord would choose to walk with me in the darkness, just like that usher. Near enough to grab an arm should I stumble, close enough to illumine a written Scripture for personal guidance or to wrap His words of comfort around my troubled heart. With God at my shoulder shining His light at my feet, I had nothing to be afraid of. Thankfully, I relaxed and enjoyed the rest of the play.

Lend Me Your Hope[49]

"God, help me make some sense out of all these tragedies, or I'll go crazy."

Hearing my anguished cry, counsellors by the dozen came forward to tell me what had gone wrong and how I could improve my life. Like Job's comforters, some added to my painful confusion; others helped ease the burden.

The counsellor who helped me the most saw me only once, in his home.

On the appointed day, his wife came to the door and ushered me into her husband's office.

After the usual pleasantries, I dove right in: "My husband's not getting any better. Every time I see him, he's worse. He can't even talk sensibly any more."

The counsellor nodded. He'd seen my husband in Riverview, in the high security ward of British Columbia's provincial psychiatric hospital. After three years of aggressive treatment, my husband's acute depression had become chronic. Several attempts at suicide had necessitated constant surveillance. He almost always wore hospital pajamas. Every treatment had failed and left him in a worse condition.

Besides trying to cope with my husband's illness and the demands of running a household single-handedly, I faced other stresses that bombarded our family of seven. In a car crash, I totalled our Volvo. A gasoline explosion sent our thirteen-year-old son to the hospital with severe burns. An older daughter was leaving home for Europe.

Illness made me miss too many days at my part-time nursing job, and my boss had sounded her displeasure. Deep personal disappointments left me wondering whom I could trust. Besides this, I was tormented by seeing my children suffer and not knowing how to comfort them when they cried, "Where is God in all this? Why isn't He answering our prayers?"

"That's what I want to know. What's going on?" I challenged the counsellor, who'd quietly listened to my out-pouring without interruption.

"I don't know," he said.

Nothing more. No platitudes of "But we know all things work together for good." No lofty expositions, such as those Job received from his friends. Just a simple "I don't know," such as a fellow pilgrim who's also baffled by life's perplexities might say.

Then he asked, "Helen, does God still love you?"

Stunned, I looked at his kind face. I wasn't prepared for this simple question.

"Yes," I stammered. "Yes, I think so."

"I once saw the hands of God," the counsellor said. "They were pierced."

Trying to substantiate my answer, I blurted, "The Bible says God's love is everlasting, so it's got to be the same whether my life is good or bad, doesn't it?"

Again, he nodded. "You can stand on this fact: God loves you and never leaves you. Knowing that, you will cope; you will not go under."

Then he smiled and said, "Now, before you go home, let's pray."

A simple prayer followed: "Father, I thank You for my sister, here. Thank You for Your great love for her. Thank You that You are with her now and always will be. Amen."

So quickly, our session was over. During the drive home, I reflected on our visit. The counsellor hadn't really answered my questions. He hadn't said very much. All he'd done is remind me that I had a refuge. And isn't that what a person lost in a raging storm needs most in life—a safe refuge where he or she will be cared for?

Throughout the years, other people—some with no counselling degree—reminded me of God's faithfulness. As long as I had God on my side, I'd be cared for. Our family would survive.

And it was so. Our son healed without a scar. My health improved. After four years in psychiatric institutions, my husband came home. However, he had a relapse and needed to return for three-and-a-half more years. With some improvement in his health, he now lives in a group home.

What have we gleaned from these experiences? Our lives are richer for having gone through this testing. We've had a chance to experience first-hand the mysteries of God's working. When life goes crazy, God does not jump in and fix it for us. He doesn't even answer our why questions. He offers Himself.

Counsellors who reminded me of this were like a window through which I could glimpse God—a refuge while the storm beat itself out, a Father who'll do the good and right thing for each of His children. In His perfect timing, deliverance comes.

He's Holding Me[50]

It's almost one hour before midnight. The streets are deserted except for a few stragglers. Trees, stripped of leaves by winter's chill, stand black against foggy street lamps. In houses, lights go out as people head for bed.

As I drive to work for the night shift at a nursing home, my mood resembles the winter night. Shouldering the responsibilities of our family alone has presented numerous challenges. Concerned friends have encouraged me to "keep hanging onto God and His promises." Like a terrified child, I've clung to the Father for months. But tonight, I feel my strength slipping. How much longer can I hold on to God's hand? And if I fall, what will happen to the children? They look to me for stability and comfort.

As I enter the warm and well-lit nursing home, I breathe a sigh of relief. *Thank God for my job as a registered nurse.* For eight hours in this other world, I can will my problems into the background.

I check on blind Mr. Isaac. In the last stages of throat cancer, he's going to need special care tonight. Propped up in bed, he struggles for breath. The raw tumour stuck in his throat is strangling him. He keeps clearing his throat, yet the obstruction does not go away. He's starved, yet afraid of the pain of swallowing. I offer him liquid morphine for the pain and Ensure for his hunger. Sitting beside him, I take his thin, veined hand in mine.

"Nurse," he croaks in a hoarse whisper, "Jesus is holding me."

A flush of joy washes over his emaciated face as I read some well-marked Scriptures to him:

"He [God] reached down from on high and took hold of me; he drew me out of deep waters."[51]

"For I am the LORD, your God, who takes hold of your right hand and says to you, Do not fear; I will help you."[52]

"Though he stumble, he will not fall, for the LORD upholds him with his hand."[53]

My reading is punctuated with his hoarse, "Yes! Yes, He's holding me."

Morning light is forcing back the night. As I drive home, I'm mulling over my encounter with blind Mr. Isaac. Could anything be worse than what he's going through right now? Yet, Mr. Isaac has found peace and strength—even joy. Why?

Slowly, it dawns on me: Mr. Isaac has discovered it's not how hard we hang on to God's hand but how tightly God hangs on to ours that counts. Yet, in my frantic efforts to keep God at my side, have I not accused Him of the possibility of letting go of me?

"Forgive me, Lord," I whisper. "From now on, I'll depend on You to hold me and each of the children."

As I lean back into the bucket seat, it seems as if I'm leaning into the arms of God. The panic of the night before is being replaced with a new optimism.

Out of the Fog

Afflicted with deep depression, I used six key ideas to focus my mind on God and take the needed steps that brought me through a deep valley. May you, too, find them helpful.

During a difficult time in my life, depression, thick as valley fog, rolled over me. For two years, despair engulfed me. God seemed a million miles away. I saw no end to the dark tunnel I found myself in.

Driving through a dense fog one night, unable to see even the white line in the middle of the street, I got a hint on how to overcome my depression. I was faced with a choice. Would I focus on the obvious fog all around me or the dim reflectors in the road? Because I wanted to get home that night, I chose to focus on the dim "bright spots" in the fog. By sheer faith, I inched ahead, from one reflector to the next. Eventually, I got to the warmth and light of home. By using the same mind-focusing principle that got me through the valley fog, I inched myself out of a crippling depression. How?

1. Soaking up music that affirms God's love and forgiveness and sends a whisper of hope behind the iron curtain of gloom. Sometimes a phrase of a song would reverberate in my mind all day long: "You lift me up when I fall down...my hope is in You alone."

2. Brisk walking or jogging. While outdoors, I'd deliberately harness my mind by focusing on my surroundings and expressing my appreciation. "I like that tree, Lord," I'd say. "Thanks for making it."

3. Copying a small Scripture of God's love and faithfulness onto a card and saying it out loud many times a day: "You, O LORD, keep my lamp burning; my God turns my darkness into light."[54] Then I'd add, "That's God's Word to me. I believe it."

4. Practising the power of positive confession. Satan wants me to doubt God and complain. So I will speak to the contrary. With my mouth, I will say, "God is good," even if I don't feel like it.

5. Keeping a record of all the good things that happened during the day: my garbage was picked up; my neighbour smiled at me; I did laundry and the machine worked well; I made supper and my family enjoyed it. At the end of the day, I would read my list and think, I had a pretty good day. Meanwhile, emotions screamed to the contrary. I realized they were not telling me the truth. Damaged emotions were not a reliable measure. Like ornery children, they were screaming and pulling me, but if I took a firm hand and said, "We're going this way," they'd come along.

6. Resisting the temptation to hide from people. The warmth and caring of sensitive people make God's love tangible—easier to grasp.

The time came when I heard the Lord Jesus whisper above my doubts, "The winter is over and spring has come.

Let Me show you." Timidly, I left my dismal prison of two years. With a stab of joy, I realized the fog had lifted and I was free! Free to follow Jesus into the sunshine of His love and new abundant life. Freer than ever before.

Depression, like winter, had served its purpose to purify and strengthen faith.

Facing Your Fear[55]

I'll never forget the day I asked my hockey buddy Curtis Klassen to come over to my house for night. It was Friday, November 17. Mom and her friend were going to spend the weekend in Grand Forks, North Dakota—about an hour and a half away from Altona, where we lived. Altona is a peaceful, predominantly Mennonite town of about 5,000 people in southern Manitoba, Canada. But, by the way Mom gave me instructions on what to do in case of an emergency, I could tell she was still nervous about leaving us two alone.

"Mom, I am fourteen," I said. "We'll be okay."

Curtis and I had met nine weeks before at WC Miller Collegiate High School. Although he was a year older and a grade ahead of me, we hit it off right away, mostly because we both played goalie for the Altona Maroons.

Curtis and his buddies went to church. I wasn't a Christian, but I went along with them. We weren't the type to get into trouble, so I couldn't understand Mom's worry.

After school, Curtis and I went to a teen dance. When we got home, we watched a movie. Shortly before midnight, I popped another video into the VCR. We had just started watching *The Hunt for Red October* when the doorbell rang.

"What's up?" Curtis asked. I shrugged my shoulders. A caller ringing the doorbell at midnight? I opened the door a crack and saw Earl Giesbrecht, a grade twelve guy from high school, standing there with a large duffle bag in his hand. He was dressed all in black.

I couldn't make out what he wanted, but then Earl was like that; you never knew how to take him. That's why the kids at school left him alone. But I'd decided I wouldn't shun him just because others did, so I said, "It's cold out there. You want to come in?"

Earl plopped himself and his bag in front of the television. We continued to watch the movie for awhile.

Then Curtis asked, "What's in the bag?"

"Tricks of the trade," Earl said.

"What does that mean?"

"I'll show you," he said. He pulled out a .357 handgun and proceeded to take out the bullets. *I've heard he stole that gun,* I thought. *What kind of a guy is he?* Earl reached into his duffle bag and pulled out a roll of hockey tape, a pair of rubber gloves, a flashlight, and a can of gasoline. Then he put everything back methodically and continued watching the rest of the movie with us.

At 1:30 a.m. it was time to go to bed, and I was wondering why Earl wasn't going home. Abruptly, he left the room. Curtis and I went to my bedroom, and we were getting ready to go to sleep when suddenly Earl barged through the door. He was pointing the gun at us. Before I could think, he threw me a roll of hockey tape. "Tie up Curt," he barked. "Hands behind his back."

My mind was in slow motion. I caught the tape. *This isn't really happening,* I thought.

I began to tape Curt's arms together behind his back. *I'm watching the ABC special. In a few moments, I can switch off this ugly scene, and we can go to bed.*

"Why are you doing this?" Curt asked.

"You'll soon know," Earl drawled. He was calm and calculated, as if he were following a carefully devised script. Then he put masking tape over Curtis's eyes.

"Take your shirt off," he told me. I did, and he tied my hands behind my back and blindfolded me. Then he ordered Curtis to go to my mother's bedroom. After awhile, he came back, pushed me to the floor, and sexually molested me.

As I lay shivering on the floor, I heard him unhook my stereo. *He's going to rob us and leave,* I thought. But he didn't leave. Instead, he went to Curtis's room. I heard banging in the closet and wondered what he was doing. Then he came back into my room. "What time is it?" I asked, thinking if I could get him talking, he might stop what he was doing.

"Four fifteen," he said.

Earl tore the masking tape off my eyes, then ordered me to kneel in front of him with my back toward him. He put his arm around my neck and yanked my head back.

"Curtis is dead," he said. "And you're next."

In a flash, he whipped out a kitchen knife and slashed my throat. Blood spurted out and ran down my bare chest. I felt a sharp pain, and then I went numb. Again, he heaved his knife into my throat. And again. I slumped to the floor, pretending I was dead.

I heard Earl leave the room; then I heard banging in the living room.

Somehow, I got up and headed for the door. He saw me. "Why won't you die!" he shouted He shoved me back into my bedroom, yanked a comforter off my bed, and threw it over me. A pungent smell of gasoline stung my nostrils; then an intense heat seared my flesh. He was burning me alive! "God, take me now," I gasped.

"Get up and go!" I heard a clear voice, not audible but in my heart.

I got to my feet and stumbled into the living room. Small fires were burning everywhere. Billows of black smoke made me choke. I got to the front door, and with hands behind my back, reached for the doorknob and twisted it. The door opened. A gulp of fresh air cleared my head. I dashed across the yard to my neighbour's house and pushed on the doorbell. It was 4:30 a.m.

Bruce Penner gasped as he saw me. I tried to tell him that our house was on fire and Curtis was in there, but I couldn't talk. All I could do was wave my arms. He brought me a piece of paper, and I wrote it down. Quickly, he stepped outside and looked. By now, smoke was coming out of the windows.

Bruce's wife Patty wound a clean tea towel around my neck while her husband called the ambulance, the police, and the fire department.

Later, at the hospital in Altona, the doctor put cold packs on my throat, gave me a saline drip, and put a tracheotomy tube into my windpipe, which was almost completely severed. Then the ambulance roared to St. Boniface Hospital in Winnipeg, where the doctors stitched up the gaping wound that had narrowly missed both jugular veins. Finally, I was transferred to the ICU burn unit at the Health Sciences Hospital. I had third-degree burns (to twenty-five percent of my body) that would need large skin grafts, held to both of my arms and my chest with hundreds of staples.

Mom and her friend Mike Klassen (who later became my stepdad) came to visit me as soon as they got the message from the Royal Canadian Mounted Police. But it wasn't until Tuesday that I gained consciousness and found out what happened to Curtis. "Curtis is dead." My mother started to cry. "They found his charred body in the house."

Curtis was dead, and I was alive. I felt grateful, but also guilty. Could I have done something to save him? What would have happened if I had died? Curtis, a Christian, went to be with the Lord. But I wasn't a Christian. I knew then, God was calling me. Still, I wasn't ready to give my life to Christ.

I was in the hospital for forty-eight days. The support we received from the church, the school, and the community was overwhelming. My room filled up with cards and banners and flowers.

Many visitors told me they were praying for me. I know that's why my skin grafts took so quickly and why, a year and a half later, my throat healed completely, even though the specialist in Toronto predicted that I'd have to keep the tracheotomy for the rest of my life and I'd probably not be able to speak again. But the most amazing recovery was the healing of my memory. I have no bad flashbacks and no fear of fire. All this happened without professional counselling.

Yes, for awhile I struggled emotionally. I asked why this happened to me. I learned it's okay to ask why, because it's part of facing the fear and dealing with what happened. But you have to move on beyond the why. You have to go on with life.

For me, going on with life included accepting Christ and declaring my firm commitment to follow Jesus the rest of my life. On Easter Sunday, four and a half years after the tragedy, I was baptized. Then, nine years after the incident, I married Jennifer Friesen. We chose Romans 8:28 for our verse: "And we know that in all things God works for the good of those who love Him." I really believe that God has brought good out of this horrible situation.

Today, I'm a professional firefighter in Vancouver, British Columbia. Why firefighting? I want to help people, and I know this is what God wants me to do. I'm very involved in raising money for the Firefighters Burn Fund, and every summer I counsel kids at camp who are burn survivors. I tell them, "When the rough times come, you can let what happened destroy you, or you can learn from it and grow."

Editor's Note:

Earl Hugh Giesbrecht is serving a life sentence in prison. His motive for attacking Curtis and Tyler is not clear.

In memory of Curtis, his mother opened a shop in Altona Mall. Petals and Wings sells flowers and angels. The angels on display look like delightful little human beings endowed with wings. To celebrate Tyler's amazing recovery, ornaments of fire trucks and firefighting gear are on display. Curtis's mother, Milly Klassen, works part-time at the shop. Every November 17th, the shop is closed in remembrance of Curtis.

Tyler Pelke

Across the Generations

Lord, you have been our dwelling place
throughout all generations.
Before the mountains were born
or you brought forth the earth and the world,
from everlasting to everlasting you are God.

PSALM 90:1,2

Youth is the gift of nature, but age is a work of art.

GARSON KANIN

If your vision is for a year, plant wheat.
If your vision is for ten years, plant trees.
If your vision is for a life time, plant people.

AN OLD CHINESE PROVERB

Live a good, honourable life. Then when you get older
and think back, you'll be able to enjoy it a second time.

AUTHOR UNKNOWN

No Room for Resentment[56]

When my great-uncle Henry—a bachelor who seldom left his home—died, his relatives came to the funeral like prospectors rushing to a gold mine. During his long and lonely life, his brother and sister had little time for him. Even now, they left all the arrangements for the funeral, transportation from the Vancouver International Airport, and the hosting of guests to our family.

After the funeral, Henry's relatives came to our home. My mother exuded warmth and comfort. Smiling, she rushed around serving coffee, buns and cheese, and tasty squares.

I remembered the many times I had seen Mother serving this family. For more than thirty years, she had cleaned Henry's house, washed his clothes, ran his errands, and taken favourite meals to him. Henry was not one to voice appreciation; he was even more reluctant to part with his money. And it seemed he had quite a fortune. We speculated what would happen upon his death. If anyone deserved to be remembered in his will, it was my mother.

After the meal, the table was cleared; the executor of the will opened the envelope and began to read Henry's last will and testament. As I listened, I couldn't believe my ears! My mother's name was not mentioned. Henry had left all his wealth to his distant and affluent brother and sister.

Stunned, I left the table and began to wash dishes—rather noisily, I might add. I was still fuming when my mother joined me and began to dry the dishes. I could tell by the look on her face that, as far as she was concerned, there was nothing amiss.

"Why aren't you resentful?" I stormed.

"Resentful?" Mother's blue eyes registered surprise. "Why, nobody made me do what I did. Henry gave me an opportunity to serve God, and I never expected pay. You see, he doesn't owe me anything."

He doesn't owe you anything! I could hardly comprehend the meaning of her words. And yet, when I saw what freedom such an attitude brought her, I envied her. No disappointments that left her reeling in resentment. No room for self-pity. No getting stuck in unpleasant circumstances. She could carry on her life as before. And in the coming days, she demonstrated that she really meant it: Henry's family was always welcome to visit in her home.

My mother's acceptance of life—the good and the bad—without rancour gave her great freedom. Of all the things my mother passed on to me, this was surely the most powerful.

More Life to Live⁵⁷

My mother sat precariously on a narrow examination table in the doctor's office, her blue hospital gown tied in the front. The surgeon examined a hard lump in her right breast; then he turned to me. "I strongly suspect cancer," he said. "I'll get her into a hospital as soon as I can."

As a nurse I'd expected as much, and yet I'd clung to the dim hope that, since there was no history of cancer in our family, the tumour might not be malignant.

Were we about to lose Mother? I shuddered. During the past two years, I'd lost my marriage, my family, my home, and my job. Was I about to lose the one person who'd supported me in it all?

Hearing the doctor's words, however, I realized I needed to focus on Mother. How would she take the news? In her eighty-six years, she'd been in hospital only once, for an overnight observation. Back in Ukraine, she'd given birth to her four children in a birthing house with a midwife attending.

On the way home, I carefully explained how the surgeon would do a biopsy first, and if the tumour was malignant, he would operate.

"I don't want an operation," my mother said with finality.

"Then you will die," I replied.

She fixed her bright blue eyes on mine. "I'm not afraid to die," she said. "I've had a good life."

I wondered how she could say that. She was born a few years before the Russian Revolution; her early childhood memories were of soldiers surging through her village and of bandits ransacking the family home. One morning, her uncle, killed by a bandit's sabre, was tossed from a hayloft to the street below.

During Stalin's terrible two-year famine, her teenage body became so weak she couldn't lift her swollen legs into bed by herself. Yet each morning, after drinking a watery "soup," she'd stumble to the fields of the collective farm to work. Finally a day came when she was too weak to get out of bed. In the evening, young girls ringed her bed and sang hymns. *I'm going to die*, she thought.

Miraculously, she survived the famine. She married my father and moved to another village. Soon, Stalin's purges robbed her of her two brothers—who were sent to labour camps in Siberia—and killed two of her uncles.

Then came the Second World War. My mother lost her husband, her home, and her country. For two years, she fled with four small children across Europe, the fighting front just behind. Often she endured her children crying from hunger and cold.

Eventually we immigrated to Canada where Mother worked as a farmhand in British Columbia until she turned sixty-five. "Mom, how did you do it?" I sometimes asked.

"Do what?"

"Live through all that turmoil."

"Lots of people were worse off than I was."

How typical of my mother. She quietly accepted whatever God sent her way. She never asked "Why me?" As far as she was concerned, she'd had a good life.

"Are you tired of living?" I now asked her.

Mother's cheeks flushed slightly. "My neighbour gave

me some bulbs," she said. "She told me the flowers are very beautiful. I want to plant them and see."

"You'd better have the operation then," I said quietly.

My mother agreed. A few days later, the surgeon performed a total mastectomy. I hurried to the hospital, wondering how I would comfort her. But when I arrived on her ward, she was not in her room.

"Where's my mother?" I asked the nurse.

"Probably gone exploring," she laughed. I began searching the corridors for a small woman in a red housecoat.

When I found her, she assured me she felt fine. But in her eyes I detected a deep weariness, and I encouraged her to go back to bed.

In her room her gaze fixed upon me. "I don't feel like a whole person any more," she said quietly.

I winced at her humiliation. "Yes, I know," I said, trying to steady my voice. "But to me you're as beautiful as you always were."

As Mother's health improved, she began working in her garden again. She planted bulbs, and geraniums, and petunias, and a myriad other flowers, rejoicing in each one that graced her garden. She carried bouquets of flowers to her church or across the street to her friends in a seniors' home.

Soon she was as busy as ever, entertaining company, helping out at church functions, and sewing for her grandchildren. I relished our time together, our intimate chats.

Almost a year later, after a thorough examination, the cancer specialist said, "I find nothing to be worried about. You need not return unless your doctor finds something suspicious again."

On the drive home, Mother was clearly relieved. But having accepted yet another trial without self-pity or bitterness, she'd already dismissed it as of no importance. "It's done me no harm," she said.

For the rest of the trip home, Mother chatted happily about future plans. There were more flowers to plant, meals to cook, clothes to sew.

As for me, I have been granted a priceless gift. With my mother to encourage and inspire me, I know now I'll get through the tough times.

A Grandson Remembers

*Oma,**

In this festive room of tables decorated with lace cloths, green mats, and bright marigolds, you will see many happy faces. Many people have come——some from great distances——to celebrate your ninetieth birthday. Why have we come? Because we want to tell you that you have enriched our lives in more ways than you realize. Let me share some of my fond memories with you now.

On a visit to your home, I remember your cheerful greetings at the door urging us to "Come on in." Then, seeing I didn't have a jacket on, you would hurry away to find a warm sweater and slippers for me to wear. "You must dress warmer," you'd chide me in a good-natured way.

I remember the amazing meals you made for us: perogies filled with cottage cheese and doused with a rich sour cream sauce; farmer sausage fried golden brown, cabbage borscht (the best I've tasted anywhere); fruit mousse with lots of prunes in it; roll kuchen eaten with

*German for *grandmother*

watermelon; and the seemingly endless supply of buns, cookies, cake, pop, and candy. When we could eat no more, we would retire, happy and relaxed, to the living room to watch a Walt Disney movie on your giant television screen.

I remember the many thoughtful Christmas gifts you made for me, rocket pajamas or knitted slippers when I was young. Now that I'm a man, and a medical doctor, I wear the white clinic jacket you made for me with great pride.

Oma, I look at you now, brimming with life and joy, and I wonder what are the secrets to living so well? Tell me, how does one stay healthy and happy for ninety years? Much of it is in God's hands, I know, but you've given me some valuable life lessons that I will strive to emulate.

You have remained physically active. At ninety years of age, you still live independently, cooking and cleaning for yourself and the many guests who pass through your doors. Besides, you look after your own garden with its many flowers. And you keep sweeping your driveway until it's spotless! Your incredible physical stamina has been a source of inspiration for me and my patients.

You have remained mentally active, reading many books of enduring quality, then telling us about them.

And who of us has not shared your excitement of "Travels in Europe" with Rick Steves?

You have been socially active in your church: singing in the choir, serving in a ladies group, and working in a relief agency, sorting and baling clothes for the poor.

You live in the present moment. You never wallow in the what ifs of the past or pine for the maybes of the future. Your faith in God, coupled with a keen sense of humour, enables you to live each day to the full, then to move on with courage and joy.

You enjoy the simple things of life. Your life isn't cluttered with fancy clothes, expensive jewellery, or the latest technological toys. Your simple home has been a sanctuary where one can go to rest, to be fed, and to be strengthened in the bonds of family and friendship.

You've modeled for me what family is all about. Although your large family represents many nationalities and religions, you've treated us all alike. You've shown us how to put our differences aside and simply be family.

Oma, I'm almost two feet taller than you are; still I look up to you with my deepest admiration. You have been a source of strength and inspiration to us all. Thank you for showing me how to live life with zest and courage.

Your loving grandson, David

A Life Well Lived

Teach us to number our days aright, that we may gain a heart of wisdom.[58]

My mother died last May at almost ninety-one years of age.

With much help from my siblings and home care nurses, I was able to nurse her in her own home during the five months of her illness (pancreatic cancer) until her death. Some afternoons when she felt a little better, I would take her for rides in the country.

She would marvel at bright dandelions on a lush, green meadow; she'd notice how neatly raspberry vines had been tied in symmetrical arches; she even remarked on the colour of the roof on a house we drove past. She found beauty in detail that I, in my busyness, scarcely noticed.

Mother had expressed a desire to see tulips before she died. So, on an afternoon, I took her to a tulip farm near Chilliwack. Steadying her thin frame on the open car door, a kerchief covering her snow-white hair, she gazed longingly at the rows of red and yellow, white and pink tulips undulating in the breeze. Was she thinking, *This is so beautiful. What must heaven be like?*

Often she would quote a hymn that expressed her longing to be with Jesus or her trust in Christ's death and resurrection for her salvation. Sometimes, after I had tucked her into bed, I would hear her singing, in her raspy voice, hymns she had sung as a child with her father. She had told me how, in the twilight, they would be sitting on the oven bench, singing as they waited for the kerosene lamps to be lit. They had sung the many stanzas from memory.

Being certain of her heavenly home, my mother faced her death courageously. She spoke freely about it and made sure all her affairs were in order. Still, she was very much in charge of her daily affairs, making sure the lawn was cut, the house was tidy, and her many guests received a cup of tea and a cookie before they left.

One day she said, "If I had known that I would not have much longer to live, I would have baked more cookies." When I laughed at this, she said, "No, seriously. I would have filled the deep-freeze with cookies—you know, the jam-filled ones the children like so well."

Oh, to live life like that! I thought. *To be grateful for every small blessing and to think of others in loving service.*

Singing in the Face of Death[59]

As a special nurse in an acute care hospital, I was primarily responsible for giving support to the dying patient and his family, and often I felt inadequate for the job.

One particular May morning, my patient, a tall man suffering from leukemia, had worsened during the night. A death-pallor lay on his handsome face. His wife was bending over him, trying to coax him to open his mouth and take a sip of the fruit juices blended with milk and egg that she had prepared for him. But he had drifted into unconsciousness and couldn't open his mouth.

"Paul!" she called to him. "Honey, can you hear me?" She put down her glass and cradled his head in her hands, "Oh, sweetheart," her voice quavered, "you've been the best husband any woman ever had." Almost as though her strong love for him would call him back, she continued passionately, "You've kept every promise you've ever made. You've made me extremely happy."

During the previous days, as I had chatted with relatives and hospital nurses, I had come to know more about this couple. Paul, a prominent lawyer, had married Susan late in life. They'd enjoyed an unusual love relationship for fifteen years. But during the past three years, his health had rapidly declined. He'd developed acute leukemia. Now cancer cells had infiltrated both lungs, already weakened by pneumonia. Death was imminent.

As I watched Susan, his wife, so distraught and anguished,

I wondered, *What can I do to bring a little comfort?* Suddenly I remembered the hymn book I had tucked into my large black purse. The previous day, Susan had told me about her husband's love for music. How, when he was well, he would sit for hours at the piano or organ playing hymns. Because of this conversation, I had brought along a hymn book, just in case.

Now, I reached for my purse and pulled out the book. Handing it to her, I said, "Susan, I brought my hymnal today. Do you think we could sing Paul's favourite hymn?"

She opened the book. "Oh, here's 'Amazing Grace,'" she gasped, "Paul's favourite." Then, turning to his unresponsive face, she said, "Honey, the nurse and I are going to sing for you."

"Amazing grace," she began. Her voice quavered and broke in giant sobs. She took a deep breath and bravely continued, "How sweet the sound." More wracking sobs. "That saved a wretch like me." Gazing on the face of her beloved husband, she managed to get through the song.

Then she chose another hymn. This time there were fewer sobs. During a third hymn, I noticed that her voice was becoming stronger.

Encouraged, we continued to sing. For the next two hours, we sang hymn after hymn. Staff nurses tiptoed in to check the intravenous and oxygen concentrator or to give medication. We scarcely noticed.

As the moments passed, something wonderful happened: there was a Presence in the room. Susan's anguished face had become relaxed and radiant. Then, with a voice full of confidence, she said, "Paul, this is not defeat. This is victory!"

It wasn't anything special that I had said or done, but in the singing of those faith-filled words Jesus Himself had come to bring His comfort.

The Power of Example

I have come to Senegal to visit my missionary daughter Esther, her husband Geoffrey, and my grandchildren Miriam, Nathan, and Philip. "Don't worry about entertaining me or showing me Senegal," I've told them. "Just take me along on your daily errands. I want to experience missionary life in Africa."

"Good. I've bought you a Senegalese outfit," my daughter says with a smile. She tells me that I will be accompanying her to the local dispensary, the homes of her friends, and outlying villages, and I need to be properly dressed for a Moslem country. As I view myself in the mirror, covered from head to toe in a lovely blue cotton, I smile. *I rather like this style.* Next, I learn to say the greetings in their beautiful Wolof language and marvel how often the words *peace* and *God* come into the conversation.

I am ready now to accompany my daughter on her errands of mission. First, she takes me to visit a sick friend at the dispensary. In a Spartan room, two women are lying on narrow beds. I hurry past the first one, who seems to be at death's door, and greet the second woman, who is at least sitting up. "Not that one," Esther calls. "This is Mumboy." With a sinking heart I return to the first woman. As my daughter speaks with the woman's husband, his face lights up. "My mother will pay for your wife's medication," she's told him. "And I will pray for her." Before we leave, she cups her hands in Senegalese style and prays earnestly for the woman's healing.

When we stop at a local market, a young man hails my daughter and engages her in animated conversation. He's pulled up his pant leg and is showing off an infected wound. "Jump into the car," my daughter says. "I'll take care of it at the house."

Day after day, the calls for help keep coming. A mother tells her she's spent over 4000 franc on medicine for her son and he's not getting better. "Can you come and see him?" she pleads.

We drive over to their compound and Esther examines him. "You must take him back to the doctor," she says. "I will come in the afternoon with my car and take you there." Another day, just as we're ready to go out, a chief and his wife arrive at the house with a sick child. Hurriedly Esther rummages through her medicine chest to see what she can give him: vitamins and worm medicine for the child and eye salve for the old chief himself.

I notice how quickly people seem to feel at home with my daughter. Whether she's engaged in a lively conversation with the vendors at the fish market, chatting with children who crowd around the vehicle, or visiting with people at their homes, eating out of a common bowl, soon there's good-natured joking and laughter. *She's in her element*, I think. *Despite the hardships, she loves living here and serving these people.*

At the end of a busy day, my daughter, her family, and I take our daily walk across harvested peanut and millet fields to the railway tracks. The crowds of needy people won't follow us here.

"Esther, what influenced you to become a missionary?" I ask her one day.

"You and Dad kept reaching out to people, like the Vietnamese boat people you became so involved with," she says. "I saw you minister cross-culturally. That blessed and challenged me and prepared me for foreign mission work."

My daughter's words surprise me, for I thought as a very active teenager she'd been too busy to notice. *How often we underestimate the power of example,* I think.

The following Sunday I see again how far-reaching a parent's actions can be. After breakfast, Esther's family and I squeeze into their Mitsubishi and drive to another village to worship with new believers. Since the service will be conducted in Wolof, a language the children do not understand, they are encouraged to bring books and toys to amuse themselves in the car.

After leaving the paved road, we follow tracks running through barren, dusty fields studded with baobab trees. Sometimes the road disappears into a sandy ravine. We skirt around it and drive past clusters of mud huts, their straw roofs, like giant cones, poking up behind sisal fences. When we reach Jida, the designated village, we stop, jump out of the car, and meet the men that have been waiting for us. A lively exchange of African greetings follows. I'm thankful that I have learned a few phrases so I can do my part. We enter a round mud hut and take our place beside nine men and one woman sitting on the floor on colorful sisal mats. An African man begins to read from 1. Corinthians, chapter 15. His words come out slowly and haltingly but clearly. He's been practicing his reading with a missionary during the week. I try to imagine what it's like for him, a new reader and very young Christian, hearing God's truths jump off the printed page.

After the Bible reading and a brief discussion, a praise and prayer session follows, also led by a Senegalese man. My daughter whispers a translation as a man speaks animatedly. "It's Mumboy's husband," she says. "He wants everyone to know that his wife has fully recovered." Warm grins and a chorus of "praise the Lord" follows this obvious answer to prayer. Another man thanks God for being able to sell his peanuts and buy a bicycle.

After the benediction, our leader dismisses us. We exit the dim interior of the hut. The bright sunlight makes me squint, but as my eyes adjust, I see a beautiful sight. Miriam, my fourteen-year-old granddaughter, and an African girl about her age are sitting on their haunches doing the family laundry. Their shy smiles, exchanged across a basin of soapy water, speak of camaraderie. And I know the service pattern has caught again.

Gems of Truth: Never Give Up

"So do not throw away your confidence; it will be richly rewarded. You need to persevere so that when you have done the will of God, you will receive what he has promised."[60]

The power of persistence is a mighty force. I saw this in my fourteen-year-old granddaughter Miriam, who lives in Senegal. For Christmas, she had been given a jigsaw puzzle. To cut down on weight, the puzzle had come to her home in Africa minus the box. As she dumped 1,000 pieces onto a card table, I wondered how she was going to manage. No picture to copy. No pattern to follow. Just a pile of pieces looking surprisingly similar.

As I watched my granddaughter bent over the pieces, sorting, grouping, and turning each piece for a possible fit, I marvelled at her persistence. And her faith. She believed that this jumble would make sense in the end; a picture would emerge. And buoyed by that knowledge, she kept at it day after day. Because Miriam persisted, she was rewarded by a beautiful Victorian painting.

Is your life like a jumbled jigsaw puzzle? You've been told that God has a wonderful plan for your life, but right now, all you see is broken pieces—broken dreams, broken health, broken relationships. A pattern? No, it looks more like a mess.

Perhaps you're tired and discouraged, like there's no fight left within you. God is your mighty anchor. He will hold fast to you so you do not lose your footing. However, you must also heed His command: "Do not throw away your confidence."

You need to persevere in faith and in obedience to God's Word. Keep your spiritual focus set on Him, believing that you can do all things through Christ who strengthens you.[61]

Successful people are people who have known their share of brokenness but they've refused to give up. They've hung onto their confidence that, in time, their faith in God's goodness will be rewarded.

Prayer: Father, even though I don't understand, I trust You. Give me strength to keep at it until I finish.

Crossing Boundaries

How beautiful on the mountains
are the feet of those who bring good news,
who proclaim peace,
who bring good tidings,
who proclaim salvation,
who say to Zion,
"Your God reigns!"

ISAIAH 52:7

To leave the world a bit better whether by a healthy child,
a garden path or a redeemed social condition,
to know even one life has breathed easier because you lived,
this is to have succeeded in life.

RALPH WALDO EMERSON

What Love Built[62]

When Susan and John Chalkias moved into their house in Cherry Ridge Estates, a subdivision outside Mission, British Columbia, Canada, they found many of their neighbours busily planting gardens, hanging pictures, and unpacking boxes. "It was easy to get to know people," Susan remembers. "Everyone was new." Soon the three Chalkias children were out riding their bikes, and Susan was looking into swimming and piano lessons for her kids.

One day in 1995, her neighbour Faith Black came over to share a letter she'd just received from her friend, Avis Rideout, a missionary who lived in Thailand. Avis described a visit to an overcrowded Thai orphanage for children born with AIDS. The place was extremely understaffed and the children in desperate need of care. Avis was particularly taken with a little girl she called Nikki. The infant was so sick doctors said she wouldn't last six months. "Let me take her home with me," Avis pleaded, and she eventually adopted the child.

Embraced by Avis's family, Nikki thrived. "Seeing what's happened to Nikki, I have made a promise to God and to myself," Avis wrote in her letter to Faith. "I am going to open an orphanage here for other babies with AIDS."

"How much would something like that cost?" Susan asked her neighbour.

"Avis says she could start one for $17,000," Faith replied.

Susan knew next to nothing about AIDS, orphanages, or

Thailand, but she didn't hesitate one moment. "Let's help!" she exclaimed.

People always raise money for basketball teams and school bands, Susan figured. Why couldn't she and her neighbours build an orphanage in Thailand?

And so they went to work. Their first project was a bottle drive. Susan and Faith went door to door in Cherry Ridge Estates with their children, collecting soda bottles and cans. Other families joined the effort, and soon the Chalkias's garage was filled. But all the aluminum and plastic didn't add up to many dollars and cents.

"After we turned everything in, we netted only $70," Susan recalls.

Next she called the local Save On, and they gave her permission to sell hot dogs in front of the drugstore. That event brought in a bit more money. Then someone suggested baking homemade apple pies and selling them, so one day the neighbours took over the Chalkias's kitchen.

Susan had forgotten to mention the pie bake to her husband before he left for his job at the Neptune Foods warehouse in Vancouver, where he operated a forklift. "When John came home, he found huge piles of apple peels in the garbage, flour dusting the kitchen floor, and seven women baking," Susan remembers. "He just sat down and started peeling!"

Because a new commuter train station was opening in the area, the neighbours saw another fundraising opportunity. On the weekend that the West Coast Express was launched, they set up a food stand at the station. "We called it the deal of the day," says Susan. "For only $4.50, people could buy a hamburger, a slice of pie, and a pop." At day's end, the neighbours had grossed a total of $2,000 toward their cause. "I thought to myself, 'We're over a tenth of the way there!'"

By then the neighbours had named themselves Nikki's Seed Society and registered as a charitable organization. When a Thai jewellery company heard of what Nikki's Seed Society was doing, they donated $15,000 worth of jewellery—beautiful, hand-painted pins and enamelled bracelets and earrings. "We mounted them on velvet and carried them in tackle boxes to sell," Susan says. "We had jewellery parties, like Tupperware parties. They were a great success."

A year from the date they started, the group had raised $24,629—far surpassing their goal. Avis Rideout was able to start her orphanage, Agape Home. Soon she was sending photos of the children to Susan. "I pored over those pictures every day," Susan says, "praying for the children and wishing I could meet them." Finally, in 1997, Susan and John went to Thailand with their children, Brydan, Karalee, and P.J., to work at Agape Home. They returned again a year later to act as interim directors for six months, and that's when they adopted Prem, an eighteen-month-old boy.

The work of Nikki's Seed Society continues under Susan's leadership. The days of bottle drives, hot dog sales, and pie bakes are gone. Today, Susan sends out hundred of brochures, seeking people to sponsor the children. Her can-do spirit energizes the organization, whether it's supporting Agape Home or starting a new orphanage in Zambia, Africa, where AIDS affects tens of thousands of babies.

Occasionally, somebody says to Susan in shocked tones, "You're taking your kids?"

"My children are quite safe," she responds with a smile. "You know what's really contagious? The feeling of helping others. It's a wonderful feeling. Once you've started, you can't stop. Like me with Nikki's Seed: I think it; I dream it; I talk it; I work at it. It's now part of me, and I think it always will be."

Susan's world has changed forever. Just how much change, Susan could not have envisioned. Ten years later, Seeds of Hope (as it is now called) fully sponsors three homes in Zambia: Buseko House (forty-two children), Samaritan's House (a hospice for HIV moms), and Felsen House (for service teams). The organization has bought fifty-five acres and is in the process of building Grace Village, which will have a boarding school for orphans, eight residences, a cafeteria, a recreational hall, some offices, and three teachers' houses. Seeds of Hope also fully supports Rachel Home (fifty children) in Myanmar. In the very near future, a team will be going into El Salvador to establish a home for orphans.

It all started when Susan thought, *We raise money for basketball teams and school bands. Why not for a missionary who wants to start an orphanage in Thailand? Why not?*[63] Check the references for more information.

Gospel from the Grave[64]

Self-employed trucker Dave Dever was hauling a load of junk to the garbage dump. He tossed an old mattress and a chair into the dump and reached for the box of books a woman had asked him to dispose of. As the box teetered on the tailgate, he hesitated. *Maybe I should keep the books,* he thought. *But then, why bother about other people's junk?* He picked up the box to heave it; then he put it back down again. *I'll keep them,* he decided. *I can always dispose of them later.* At home, he carried the box in his basement and forgot all about them.

One cold winter evening, Dave was stoking the fire in the fireplace. The fire needed some help, so he dumped some books from the box into it.

"What are you doing?" his wife, Abby, yelled. "Those are worth money." She grabbed the prongs and fished out three of the books.

Her husband dusted one of the volumes off and turned it over. The faded letters on the spine read: *John G. Paton, Missionary to the New Hebrides, an Autobiography.* Before long, Dave was engrossed in the tale of an amazing adventure that took place almost 150 years ago.

John Paton left Scotland for New Hebrides in the South Pacific in 1858. Friends warned him of the danger of going to a tribe of cannibals. Undeterred, Paton and Mary Ann, his young wife, made the treacherous sea voyage to Australia and then on to Tanna, one of eighty-three islands that made up New Hebrides. Four months after their arrival in Port Resolution, Mary Ann died of malaria. Their infant son died soon after. Alone, often ill, and in constant danger from hostile natives, Paton persevered to preach the gospel, to teach methods of survival, and to minister to the sick.

Dave closed his eyes and tried to imagine what it would be like to live under the threat of death twenty-four hours a day and still keep going. John Paton had courage and passion. His life counted for something.

Dave put the book down and stared into the fire. How different his life was. He got up in the morning, worked a few hours as a self-employed trucker, came home to a comfortable house, and went to sleep at night. Then he did it all over again. Yes, he was providing a comfortable living for Abby and their two children, but there had to be more to life. *I wish I could do something significant for God*, he thought. But what could he do, a trucker who had barely made it through high school? Still, as he read Paton's story again and again, hope stirred within him.

"How about a trip to Vanuatu on our twentieth wedding anniversary?" he asked Abby.

"Couldn't we just go to Hawaii?" she countered. They had never travelled overseas before, she said. There would be shots and anti-malaria medication. Besides, it was too expensive, she said.

These were perfectly logical objections. Still Dave couldn't let go of his dream. He researched Vanuatu on the Internet and subscribed to the *Lonely Planet Guide*. Seeing his enthusiasm, Abby warmed up to the idea. In June 2001, the Devers set out on the adventure of a lifetime.

First, they flew to Australia. Then they had a three-hour flight from Sydney to Port Vila, Vanuatu's capital city on Efate Island. As they exited the airplane, they stepped into a pounding rain. The airport was dark. Moments later, they were in the back seat of a taxi—backpacks up to their chins—careening at terrific speed around mud puddles and down dark streets. After a short ferry ride, a guide escorted them by flashlight down a bush trail to a rundown resort. The following morning, it was still pouring. Dave and Abby went for a walk. They couldn't have felt more out of place. Home seemed millions of miles away.

Dave wanted to find the graves of John Paton's wife and infant son, but when he mentioned the island of Tanna to a tourist guide, she shook her head. "Tanna is no place for tourists," she said. "It's too primitive."

"We've come this far," Dave said to Abby, "We can't stop now."

Putting their fears aside, they boarded a twin-engined plane. An hour later, they arrived on Tanna. What they found was far removed from Paton's memoir. Instead of warring tribes, they met many Christians, who welcomed them with wide smiles and hearty handshakes.

At an open-air church meeting in a clearing in the jungle, about 200 people were singing and dancing. Women sat on mats on the ground during the sermon. The pastor asked Dave to give a greeting. Emotion overcame him as he looked into their eager faces. "I'm not worthy to be here," he said. Then he told them about John Paton's book and how, because of the power of the gospel, they now shared the same hope in Jesus Christ.

"Praise the Master!" the congregation chorused. "Praise the Master."

At Port Resolution, Dave again asked about Mary Ann Paton's grave, but nobody knew where it was. Disappointed, he went for a walk by the seashore. He saw a man fishing and felt compelled to speak with him. The man was Chief Narua of Port Resolution. He knew where the graves were. Excitedly, Dave called Abby.

Chief Narua guided them along an overgrown footpath that led up a hill. At the top, he pointed to two graves. Mary Ann's grave, which her husband had dug near their house, had a cement foundation covered with crushed coral. Beside it, a smaller grave marked the resting place of their infant son. Tears blurred Dave's vision as he remembered Paton's words: "But for Jesus and His fellowship, I must have gone mad and died beside that lonely grave."

On the trail back to the truck, Dave, with the help of an interpreter, began telling Chief Narua about John Paton. He related how a hurricane had hit the island. A group of chiefs, believing the missionary's God had caused the disaster, decided Paton should die. They marched around his hut all night. In the morning, the chiefs were gone. They had been frightened away by "shining men with drawn swords" surrounding Paton's house. The missionary praised God for answering his prayer by sending his angelic host to protect him.

"Who were the chiefs that came to the missionary's house?" Chief Narua asked.

"Miaki, Nowar—"

The chief's eyes widened. "Nowar?" he exclaimed. He dropped to his knees and began drawing circles on the ground—five circles to show five generations. Excitedly, he told them that Nowar was his great-great-grandfather. The Devers stared at each other in disbelief. Something truly amazing was going on here.

"John Paton thought highly of Chief Nowar," Dave said. "Nowar saved his life on several occasions, by bringing him food or standing by him in great danger. In fact, Paton described your great-great-grandfather as his friend."

The chief beamed his pleasure.

In their travels throughout Tanna, the Devers noticed very few Bislama Bibles. When he showed his personal copy to two young girls, they began to read the words in their own rich tongue. Enthusiastically, they exclaimed, "This is good. This is good." Pastors also expressed a longing to own Bibles but said they couldn't afford to buy them.

The Devers resolved to raise money for Bislama Bibles. "We started with twenty-five cents," Dave said. "In time, God multiplied this seed money through our community, Sunday school, interested friends, and churches." Since that anniversary trip, Dave has returned four more times to the island of Tanna and surrounding islands, bringing almost 2,000 Bislama Bibles.

A native pastor, holding his very own Bible, exclaimed with joy, "Praise the Master! Never before have Bibles come for free to this island."

What about Chief Narua? He committed his life to Christ before his death. Each time Dave goes, he hears of other Tannese who have left their animistic and cult beliefs and have begun to read the Bible in their own language.

A book written 118 years ago changed the course of Dave Dever's life. "To see people come to know Christ is the greatest thrill of my life," Dave says. "We're reaping what Paton faithfully sowed almost 150 years ago. That's the awesome power of the gospel."[65] Check the references for more information.

Vanuatu,	formerly New Hebrides, means "Land Eternal," a country in the south Pacific made up of eighty-three islands.
Location:	Between Fiji and Australia
Capital:	Port Vila
Population:	190,000+
Languages:	English, French, Bislama, plus over 100 other languages

Forgiveness

"Though the mountains be shaken
and the hills be removed,
yet my unfailing love for you will not be shaken
nor my covenant of peace be removed,"
says the Lord, who has compassion on you.

ISAIAH 54:10

Give the following gifts:

To your enemy...forgiveness,
To your opponent...tolerance.
To a friend...your heart.
To a customer...service.
To all men...charity.
To every child...a good example
To yourself...respect

AUTHOR UNKNOWN

The brightest future will always be based on a forgotten past; you can't go forward in life until you let go of your past failures and heartaches.

AUTHOR UNKNOWN

Forgiveness doesn't change history; it makes living with it easier.

AUTHOR UNKNOWN

Finally Free[66]

Growing up in a strict Christian home in southern Germany, I thought I knew what it meant to be a Christian.

But when I entered trade school, I decided it was time to put aside the old-fashioned ways. I grew my hair long, pierced my ears, started to smoke and drink, and ran with my friends from work. I figured God wasn't relevant to my present life; in fact, He was boring.

My peers coaxed me, "Hey, Armin, stealing's no big deal."

"Everybody does it. The government steals taxes!"

The first time I sneaked a marzipan from a store, my heart beat wildly. *They'll arrest me!* I thought. I was sure of it. But soon, stealing became an exciting game. I could not leave a store without taking something.

I loved the challenge of getting something for nothing. It was fun to outwit the clerks. During those three or four months, I stole 1,000 deutsche marks' worth of merchandise—and nobody ever found out.

In March 1993, I attended "ProChrist'93," a Billy Graham crusade in Germany. As I listened to the sermon, I felt a tug at my heart. "God loves you," Billy Graham said. Wow! I'd always thought of God as an authoritarian Person ready to zap me, not as a Friend. "Come to Jesus, He'll forgive you," Mr. Graham invited. "Jesus died for your sins."

When the invitation was given, I went forward and gave my life to Christ. My parents were elated. "Now Armin will change," they said. But I couldn't live up to their expectations, and I drifted away from Christ. Still, something had changed that night; I didn't want to steal any more, and I started going to church again.

About that time, I met Benjy Thomas, who had accepted Christ also. Often we read the Bible and talked about what it meant to be a Christian—not keeping a bunch of rules, but following Jesus. We didn't change overnight. We continued to drink, smoke, and run around. I knew that my sins were forgiven, but I didn't have peace. "Lord Jesus, why can't I get close to You?" I prayed.

One day, I understood why. The thought was clear, as though God had spoken: "Armin, going to church won't make it better. I hate sin. You must get rid of the sin in your life."

Immediately the things I had stolen flashed before my eyes. But what could I do about things I'd stolen three years ago? Most had been lost or wrecked. I decided to forget about it.

God kept working on other areas of my life as well. One day, I asked myself, "Does being drunk bring me closer to Jesus?" No. Benjy and I agreed on that. "Then why do it?" So I quit getting drunk. Some months later, I quit smoking. I saw it as a bondage I could do without. Next, I realized that true love waits until marriage, so I stopped taking girls to bed.

Niggling at the back of my mind was the thought, *Someday I have to go back to those stores and make it right,* but I felt terrified. I thought I'd probably land in jail.

One day, I called two of my best friends and said, "Today I'll do it. Come with me to the stores." While Benjy and Daniel prayed outside, I stumbled into the store where I owed the smallest debt, and I asked for the manager.

"Why?" the clerk demanded.

"Three years ago, I stole some jeans. Now I want to pay for them."

The woman's mouth dropped open. "Why?" she gasped.

"My conscience bothers me."

Her eyes flashed with amusement. The corners of her mouth curled up.

"Tell you what," she said. "The manager is not in. She'll never know, because I won't tell. So go home now."

I stared at her. Had I come for this? "No," I mumbled. "I can't forget." Then I thrust a piece of paper at her. "Here's my name and address and phone number. I want to pay up."

That day we went to five stores. It didn't get any easier. Some managers agreed that I could pay back on an installment plan.

When I entered the last store, such an enormous *angst* came over me that I thought I would faint. I owed 500 deutsche marks!

"Hello," I said to the manager. "Three years ago, I stole stuff from your store. Here's some of it." I dumped a bag onto the counter.

The man looked stunned. He opened his mouth to say something, but I wedged in, "This isn't all. I stole 500 deutsche marks' worth of merchandise."

The man's face turned crimson. His eyes bulged. His mouth twitched. Then he stammered, "Wait right here."

I thought, "He's gone to call the police."

Moments later I heard his agitated voice tell everyone within earshot what I had done. Clerks and customers stopped and stared at me, contempt filling their eyes. I imagined they were shouting at me "Thief! Thief!" I burned with shame at the humiliation.

Suddenly, I felt as though Somebody had covered me. The comfort reminded me of one cold winter's day long ago when my mother had come outside and draped a coat over me. I knew that this time it was Jesus. He whispered, "It's okay Armin. I'm here with you."

When the manager returned, he was scratching his bald head. "I've never had this happen before."

"You can call the police," I said.

"Why are you doing this?" he demanded.

"I want to follow Jesus, " I said. "He has shown me it's wrong to steal."

The man blinked. His eyes got shiny and moist. "Okay. You may go."

What? I couldn't believe what I was hearing. "I'll pay," I stammered.

"*Schon gut*," he waved a large hand. "You go home."

Stunned, I managed to stammer, "May God bless you, sir."

I could have done a cartwheel out of that store—500 deutsche marks forgiven. Incredible!

I knew that God had forgiven me in full long ago, but going back to the stores and making it right just made my forgiveness seem more real. "I'm free!" I whooped. "Really free!"

Daniel and Benjy agreed. Following Jesus beats every other excitement that we had known while running with the crowd. Doing things God's way really works.

Armin Schowalter

A Girl and a Fish Hook

After the end of the Korean War, Stephanie was conceived by the union of a Korean woman with an American soldier, probably in the city of Pusan. As a child of mixed blood, she was considered a non-person. She was abandoned at about the age of four and began living on the streets. Many orphaned children of mixed blood were killed; others were picked off the streets and sent to America by adoption agencies. She wasn't.

Stephanie learned to snatch morsels from food stalls, to be at butcher shops when they threw out the bones, and to roast grasshoppers on a rice straw. At night, she'd roll herself into a straw mat and sleep under a bridge.

Even street children taunted and tormented her. Once she was tied to a water wheel and nearly drowned. Another time, she was thrown down an abandoned well. Her fingers caught on to a stone sticking out of the wall, and she hoisted herself onto it. She screamed for help until she had no more voice. Then, cold and numb, she hugged her skinny knees and watched as the patch of light at the top turned to darkness. Eventually an old woman came to the well and hauled her up, then hid her in a barn. In the morning, she told her to flee into the mountains. That night, huddling alone at the mouth of a cave, Stephanie peered out at the stars. *Why am I so bad that people want to kill me?* She wondered. *Why can't I be like other children who have a mommy and a daddy?* She left the mountain cave and began wandering from village to village, looking for food and shelter.

Stephanie was about seven when a cholera epidemic swept Korea. One day, she fainted in the street. When she woke up, she was lying on a mat in a bright room. As she sat up, she saw the room was filled with small children. A Swedish nurse had brought her to the World Vision orphanage in Taejon. She recovered and was soon strong enough to wash diapers and help feed and care for the babies at the home.

One day, an American couple came to the orphanage. David and Judy Merwin's heart went out to the little girl with the big, sad eyes, and they adopted her. When it was time to return to America, they took her with them. Her parents provided the best home life and the best education, but still Stephanie felt unloved and unlovely. Although she had prayed to receive Jesus Christ as her personal Saviour, she couldn't grasp His love. She couldn't believe that anybody could love her, a half-breed. "Think of the life of Jesus, Stephanie," her father said. "He was born in hard circumstances. Straw was His blanket, and He had to flee because some people wanted to kill Him. He was despised and rejected by His own people. Jesus knows how you feel. He has walked in your shoes."

As Stephanie thought about Jesus, something cold and brittle deep inside began to crack. For the first time in her life, she began to weep, for Jesus, who had to die on the cross, and for herself, who had never known love in her childhood. She began to share her testimony at various church functions. But when a Korean church invited her to speak, she firmly refused. Oh, she had prayed a prayer of forgiveness for all who had hurt her. Still, she could not shake a deep dislike of anything Korean. *I didn't deserve that abuse. The least they could have done is give me a decent childhood,* she thought bitterly.

Her adopted father sensed a spirit of bitterness in his daughter. But how could he talk to her about it without hurting her fragile self-esteem? He prayed for wisdom and an opportunity.

Stephanie loved to go fishing with her father. One day, she hooked a five-pound trout.

As he watched his daughter expertly pulling the fish toward the boat—sometimes letting out the line, other times pulling it taut—her father found a way to broach the subject. He waited for his daughter to land the fish safely in the boat, then he said softly, "Stephanie, when you had your hook in that fish, who controlled it?"

"I guess I did," she replied. Wondering where this conversation was going, she looked up at her father.

"Sometimes there's a hook inside us, too," her father continued. "The *you-owe-me* hook."

He looked off into the quiet expanse of lake, then back at his daughter. "I think there's resentment in your heart towards the people in Korea. Resentment has a hook that leads you in a direction you don't want to go."

As they talked, Stephanie began to see that, although she had verbally forgiven her abusers, she had tenaciously clung to the injustices suffered during her childhood. Her father was right. She did have a *you-owe-me* hook inside her heart, and it was colouring her present relationships. It was hindering her from experiencing more of the love of God. Later, in the privacy of her bedroom, she prayed a prayer of relinquishment: "Lord Jesus, I parcel up the suffering of my childhood and give it to You as an offering. Please take out the hook of resentment. I want to love You more, and I want to love all people as You love them, even Koreans."

Next time an invitation came to speak in a Korean church, acting upon her resolve to forgive, Stephanie accepted. As she told her story, people were deeply embarrassed by what had happened. "We were all victims," Stephanie tells them. "But by God's grace, we've become victors. We are free to love and be loved."

Snow White[67]

Everybody at the mission base crowded around the team that had just returned from an outreach on the streets and beach.

"Great stuff!"

"Awesome!"

"What happened next?"

You could feel the excitement in the air. As usual, I stood on the fringe, fighting off panic. *What am I doing here? I don't belong in this group. These kids have their act together; I don't.* I pulled at my big sundress, draped awkwardly over an eight-month-pregnancy bulge. I had messed up; everybody could see that. Suddenly I had an uncontrollable urge to get away. I dashed to my room and flopped on my bed. "God, You say You've forgiven me," I sobbed, "but I don't feel forgiven. I feel so dirty, so ugly." I reached for some tissue. "God, I feel so useless."

Back home in Dawson Creek, British Columbia, Canada, when my acceptance letter had come from the mission, I was psyched. After high school, I worked a year to save up money to go. A couple of weeks before I was to leave, I went to my doctor for a physical checkup. I had been feeling ill lately and thought the doctor would give me some medicine for it. Instead, he gave me a pregnancy test. I came back a week later for the results.

"Your test is positive," the doctor said.

I burst into tears. "That will ruin everything."

The doctor listened kindly. "You could have an abortion," he said. "I'll set up an appointment."

"That's not the answer," I sniffled.

Dazed, I stepped out of the doctor's office into the frigid February air. A few minutes earlier, the sun had been shining. The day had been bright with promise. Now everything was changed.

In high school, I had always felt like a nobody. I had no special talents. I had failed some courses and had to make them up. Unlike some of my classmates, I had no great ambitions for my life. The one thing I wanted more than anything else was to do an extended missions service overseas and then get married someday. But getting pregnant had killed everything.

I had to talk to somebody. Ida, a woman in our church, had been a spiritual counsellor to me before. I went straight to her house.

"Why did God let this happen to me?" I choked.

I told Ida how I'd broken off the relationship with my boyfriend because I felt what we were doing was wrong, how I had asked God to forgive me, and how I wanted to serve God with my life. "But my life is ruined now," I cried.

Ida handed me a box of tissue. "If you're going to play around, you're going to get caught," she said in her usual brusque manner. "But never mind; life goes on."

She poured two cups of tea and sat down at the table with me.

"Have you told your parents?"

"Not yet."

"That comes next," she said kindly.

I knew my parents would be shocked. In fact, everybody in our church and small community would be shocked. I was Susan, the good Christian girl, who always kept herself out of trouble—until now.

As I approached our home, I could see Mother bustling about in the kitchen. Dad was away at work. "Mom, I've got something to tell you," I said. "Come, sit down in the living room."

Mom finished what she was doing, then joined me on the sofa.

"I'm pregnant," I blurted out.

She looked at me as if I were speaking Greek.

"You're kidding," she said.

"No, Mom, this is serious." I began to cry.

Before long, Mom was crying too.

The next morning, my father phoned me at my apartment. "Susan, I hear you're in trouble," he said. "I just wanted to phone and let you know I love you."

Both my parents were incredibly accepting and supportive. They had taught me that when you do wrong, you admit it and take responsibility for it. Then God's forgiveness and healing can come. Now my mother urged me to tell the pastor and the elders of our church.

The whole world has to know that Susan sinned, I pined to myself. But I did tell the pastor and elders. They forgave me also and urged the congregation to accept me. And they did.

But most surprising of all was the mission's response to my letter. I had written and told them about my situation. I explained that I understood they wouldn't be able to accept me now and that I wanted my place to be given to somebody else. Instead they wrote, "We want you to come." I blinked. *I'm not reading this right,* I thought. But it was true. A few days later, I received a phone call from the mission asking me to come.

So the following spring I began my seven months of service. Although the staff and my coworkers tried hard to make me feel accepted, I felt different. *They're just being nice because they're supposed to,* I thought. *Deep inside, they wish I hadn't come. I'm an embarrassment to the team.*

The girls in the mission gave me a baby shower. In each

small gift, I had found a Bible verse assuring me of God's love. That should have encouraged me, but it didn't. *God loves me because He has to,* I reasoned. *After all, He loves the whole world. But God doesn't like me. How could He?*

Now, on my knees in my bedroom, I told God, "Coming on this mission trip was a crazy idea. I can't share my faith with anybody. Nobody will want to listen to me. They'll take one look at my swollen stomach and say, 'Who do you think you are, talking about God?'"

The next morning during my quiet time, I had a strong feeling that God had someone in particular for me to talk to that day. As my partner and I stepped out of our hotel, I felt excited.

As we walked along, I saw a man, about forty-five, sitting on a bench, reading a newspaper. Somehow I knew that he was the one. I stopped dead in my tracks. *God, You want me to talk to him?* The same strong feeling I'd had earlier returned. Timidly, I sat down on the far side of the bench and glanced at the man. His face remained buried in the newspaper.

"Sir, can we talk?" I stammered.

He kept on reading his paper as though he hadn't heard me. My heart pounded. My face flushed. My palms got sweaty.

"Sir, I'd like to talk to you." I repeated.

The man didn't budge. Clearly he wanted to be left alone. I got up to leave. Again, the old doubts washed over me. Who did I think I was, presuming to hear the voice of God? Of course, a man wouldn't want to listen to me. But as I walked away, I felt a strong impression that God wanted me to speak with that man. *All right, God, I'll try once more.* I sat down again.

"Excuse me, sir. God has told me that I am to talk to you," I blurted out.

He dropped his newspaper. His steel-grey eyes scanned my flushed face, then flitted across the bulge under my loose dress and rested on my left hand.

I could feel his annoyance. "Who do you think you are?" he scoffed. "God has told you to speak to me?" He cleared his throat. "I bet you're not even married."

I became flustered. *What do I tell him?*

The truth.

"You're right, I'm not married," I said. "I know what I did was wrong, but God has forgiven me."

The man stared at me, his mouth a tight line. His lips began to quiver. His eyes became moist. Then he started to cry, big shoulder-heaving sobs. Not knowing what to say, I just sat there. Finally, the man pulled a checkered hanky from his pocket and blew his nose. In a husky voice, he said, "I have a daughter about your age. She serves God like you— sings with a Christian musical group."

"You must be very proud of her," I mumbled.

His eyes filled with pain. "My daughter got pregnant in high school. I made her get an abortion."

"I'm sure she's forgiven you, sir."

The man stiffened. He balled his hands together. "I haven't been to church since."

"God has forgiven you, too, if you've asked Him to," I said.

"But I can't forgive." His face twisted, as if he were going to cry again.

"You don't have to feel guilty forever," I said.

The man jumped up, his newspaper falling onto the sand. He turned and walked briskly toward the hotel.

I jumped up too and ran after him. "Sir, God has forgiven you," I yelled. "Please believe that."

As I continued to walk along the beach, I thought about

my conversation with the man. I hadn't known what to say to him, but God had. The man had touched my worst fear; I had faced it and told him the truth. And what was the truth? That I had messed up but God had forgiven me, and that he didn't have to feel guilty forever.

Hey, that's for me, too! I almost shouted out the words. In the days and weeks to come, the reality of God's complete forgiveness worked its way into my heart. I'm clean, not because I've never sinned but because Jesus Christ has washed me. "Though your sins are like scarlet, they shall be as white as snow."[68] For the first time in months, I felt clean.

When my daughter was born, I named her Thalea, Greek for "a flower beginning to open up." Thalea was the joy of my life, but being a single parent was tough. Often, as I watched couples play with their children, my heart would almost break. Even though God had forgiven my sin, I felt unworthy of marriage. I regretted that Thalea would never have the joy of having two parents. But God had a better idea. He brought a man into my life who wanted to be my husband and Thalea's father.

Some people said that, because of my sin, I couldn't be married in white; it wouldn't be a good example to the younger girls of the church. At one time, I would have agreed with them.

My wedding day arrived, and as the organ played and my family and friends looked on, I glided down the aisle of the church, my dress long and white. It was not, after all, a day to dwell on my failures but a day to celebrate God's grace in my life. I was as clean, as pure, as any bride could be, not because I had never sinned but because Jesus Christ had washed me and made me white, white as snow.

Susan Houle

*My Life Is Ruined[69]

Oh God, please let it be negative. I repeated my prayer over and over as my mom and I neared the doctor's office. I usually had no trouble talking to my mother, but today we rode in silence. We both knew this trip to the doctor could change our lives forever. As I stared out the car window, I continued my plea: *God, please don't punish me for one mistake.*

Mom stayed in the waiting room as the nurse called me inside. After the doctor asked me a few questions, a nurse did a pregnancy test. Then, I went back into the waiting room and slumped down beside my mother. We thumbed through tattered magazines, but I couldn't concentrate. *God, You've got to help me.*

I guess we waited about fifteen minutes, but it seemed like forever to me. Finally a nurse stepped through the door and called my name. This time, Mom got up, too, and followed me.

"Positive," the doctor said. "In eight months, you'll be a mother."

A mother! I'd always wanted to be married someday and be a mother, but not *now*. I wished the doctor had said, "In eight months, you'll be dead."

In the car, Mom didn't say a word. I cried all the way home, then dashed into my room and flopped onto my bed. "My life is ruined," I moaned.

*All names have been changed.

My thoughts turned first to suicide and then abortion, but I knew they weren't true options for me.

"Why didn't You stop it from happening, God?" I cried.

Bob and I were in the ninth grade at a Christian school. I was captain of the cheerleading squad, and Bob played centre on the basketball team. As I'd yell out cheers, my eyes followed his well-conditioned body dribbling the ball in perfect rhythm across the gym floor.

Soon, Bob noticed me, too. "Hey," he'd call out, after a game. When we'd meet in the hall at school, he'd flash me a big grin. "How's it going?"

Eventually, our greetings turned into conversations. We'd walk to class together, and if he hadn't seen me for a day, he'd call me at home. "Just missed you," he'd say. I loved his wit, his thoughtfulness, his laughter.

In the following weeks Bob and I spent a lot of time together. Soon our friendship blossomed into romance. We'd spend every weekend together at the movies, some church concert, or just hanging out.

One weekend, I babysat my pastor's two children overnight at their home, and Bob joined me. After the kids were in bed, we cuddled on the couch and talked as usual. But then Bob's hand slid across my body and began to fumble with my clothes. I knew what we were doing was wrong, but I didn't want to hurt Bob's feelings. Besides, I didn't want him to think that I was weird.

But the next morning, I felt dirty, guilty, and scared. I couldn't look at Bob. He must have felt the strain too, for he avoided me. Nothing was the same after that. Now, weeks later, I knew nothing would ever be the same again.

The day after I'd been to the doctor, I phoned Bob. "Guess what? I'm pregnant."

"Come off it," he laughed. "Don't tease me like that."

When he found out I wasn't kidding, he blurted out, "We'll get married then."

"No way," I said. "We can't get married."

From then on, Bob didn't phone any more, and he didn't return my calls. At school, he avoided me. When we finally met in the hall one day, he looked down at the floor. "I guess we messed up," he said.

"I'm sorry," was all I could say.

Soon after, he left the Christian school and went to a public school.

I stayed at the Christian school until I started showing. Then I had to leave—that was the rule. I felt like an outcast. I felt as if nobody would ever love me again.

I began attending special classes for pregnant girls at a public school in the afternoon. All the girls in my class talked about keeping their babies, and I joined right in. We'd love our babies and take good care of them. I could visualize my darling child as I'd bathe him and dress him and take him for a walk in the stroller. I'd read to him and buy special toys. We'd be friends for life.

But sometimes I thought, *I want to finish high school. How am I going to find money for daycare and all the stuff we'll need?* When such doubts nagged me, I prayed to Jesus to make me a good mother and help me find a way. *I'll manage somehow*, I'd say to myself.

Four months into my pregnancy, my mom took me to a Christian adoption centre. The counsellor worked out on paper how much money it would cost for the first year of my baby's life: diapers, baby food, clothes, furniture, toys, day-care. I stared at the astronomical figure in dollars and cents. I was sixteen now. I worked after school, but what I earned hardly paid for gas for my car. I knew my mother couldn't help out financially. Then the counsellor said, "Babies need twenty-four-hour care, every single day. Are you prepared to give him that much time and energy?"

I resented her being that blunt. As a Christian, didn't I just have to trust God? Wouldn't God take care of all my needs? Then I remembered God hadn't stopped this pregnancy. Although God had forgiven me, He hadn't protected me from the natural consequences. Maybe looking after a baby was like that. God wouldn't do any miracles there either but would expect me to take full responsibility.

"I'm not telling you what to do," the counsellor said. "Just take a good look at what's involved. Ask yourself, 'What can I give this baby? What can I not give this baby? What is best for the baby's future?'"

When I asked Mom what she thought I should do, she said, "It's your decision. Think and pray about it. God will guide you."

At night, I couldn't sleep. I tossed and turned as I tried to decide what to do. I wanted to keep my baby. How could I give him up? Would anybody else love my child the way I did? I'd always wanted to be a mother and have a child to care for. But did I have the resources at this time in my life to look after him? I visualized this baby growing up. He'd need clothes and food and twenty-four-hour care. What kind of a future could I promise my child? Was it fair to keep my baby just because of my emotional ties to it? *Oh God, this is so hard. I don't know what to do.*

I switched on the light and grabbed my Bible. Propping myself up with pillows, I began to read Psalm 139: "For you created my inmost being; you knit me together in my mother's womb...your eyes saw my unformed body. All the days ordained for me were written in your book..." (verses 13-16).

Somehow I knew these words were for both me and my baby. Although I'd messed up, God was bigger than my failures. God was still in control. He had a plan for my baby, no matter what I decided.

My thoughts turned to adoption again. What if God had picked out two parents for my child—a man and a woman who'd been yearning for a child and couldn't have one? I tried to visualize their happy faces as I placed my baby into their arms. I tried to imagine how they'd care for his every need. Perhaps by letting go, I would be showing my baby that I loved him even more than I loved myself.

In the morning, I told my mom I had decided to place my baby up for adoption. Several months later, I gave birth to Jordan, a healthy boy, weighing seven pounds, one ounce. As I held him, tears of joy flooded my eyes. What a miracle! What a precious gift of life!

For three days, I held and fed my baby. He was perfect— he had lots of black hair, a round, pudgy face, and blue eyes. As I played with his little hands and feet, I tried not to think about giving him up.

The day the nurse came to pick him up she said softly, "It's time to say goodbye to Jordan." As I held him close, my heart pounded; tears stung my eyes. I wanted the nurse to go away, but I knew the time had come to let go. I kissed Jordan on his little forehead, then handed him to her.

After I watched the nurse leave the room with Jordan in her arms, I wanted to scream, "Wait, come back," but instead I rolled over to face the wall and sobbed uncontrollably. I knew I would always love my son no matter what. I would never forget him.

That was a few years ago. I don't know where Jordan is today. After those three days in the hospital, I never saw him again. But I have his photo on my fridge, and every day I pray for him.

Giving up Jordan was the hardest thing I've done in my

life, but I still think it was the right choice. Placing his needs above my own desires was the most loving thing to do. I definitely wouldn't choose to go through that kind of pain again, but I'm thankful for what God taught me through it. He showed me that even when I mess up, He is faithful. He can take even my sin, and turn it into something beautiful—like Jordan.

That is truly a miracle.

Tracy Anderson

It's Not Fair![70]

Visiting my dad in the provincial psychiatric hospital had always filled me with dread. But on that drizzly day in December, as I mounted the massive stairway to the front entrance, I was excited. I had important news for my dad: in less than a week, I'd be leaving for Switzerland to study at a discipleship training school. He'd be so proud of me when he found out how I earned the money myself and made all my own travel plans.

As Mom and I entered the smoke-filled lounge, we saw Dad sitting stiffly in a worn armchair beside a scruffy-looking Christmas tree. A television blared in a corner. Patients shuffled about the room or sat on the floor.

"Hi, Dad!" I said as cheerily as I could.

He turned his head in my direction. No smile; no glint in his eyes that said, "I'm glad you've come." Only pain showed in his grey eyes. He motioned for us to sit down.

"Dad, I'm leaving home for seven months," I began.

No comment. *Hasn't he heard me?* "Dad, you know the Youth With a Mission school in Lausanne? Well, I'm going to study there."

He fastened his grey eyes on me. Not a spark of interest. Not a single question. Instead, Dad picked up a worn magazine and began to turn the pages.

Disappointment flooded me. Then rage. Dad might as well have slapped me hard across my face.

Driving home in the car, I yelled at my mom, "Why does

he have to be so mean? Why can't he show a bit of interest in me at least once?"

Mom tried to tell me Dad's severe depression had frozen his emotions, but I couldn't accept her excuses for his behaviour.

"Every time I tell him anything about me, he acts as though he couldn't care less. He doesn't care that I played Marilla in *Anne of Green Gables*. He doesn't care that I lettered in soccer. He doesn't care that I graduated with honours and got a scholarship. He doesn't care that I'm leaving and won't see him for seven months. All he cares about is himself."

A few days later, when I boarded the KLM jet, I felt a bit scared. But mostly I felt relief. Visiting Dad in that dreadful hospital would not be part of my life any more. I could now forget the pain of his rejections and get on with my life.

When I arrived at the discipleship training school, I couldn't believe the way people welcomed me. Their eyes filled with interest when I answered their questions about myself. Their voices were full of caring.

Soon, my three roommates and I felt as if we'd known each other forever, and yet it was only a few weeks. After classes, we'd take trips on a bus down the hill to a quaint village, or explore the shores of Lake Geneva, surrounded by grape vineyards and framed by majestic mountains, or wander into the small woods behind the school where we could do exercises at fitness stations.

I enjoyed my classes. I was getting along great with my new friends. Every day held a special adventure. Still, I dreaded the time when small prayer groups were held after lunch.

An older staff person would encourage us to share specific needs in our lives. I knew I ought to say something about my dad, but I couldn't.

It came as a total shock one day when our leader prayed,

"God, release Cathy from the hurt in her life. Help her to forgive the person who's hurt her."

I began to shake. My head felt stuffed. I fumbled around for a tissue. Quietly our leader handed me one and gave my hand a squeeze.

Later, I told her about my dad. "He used to be at every single basketball game my brother and sister played in," I choked. "He cheered so loudly that my mom tried to shush him up. But he's not been to even one of my soccer games."

"How long has your dad been depressed like this?"

"Four years."

"Cathy, you feel cheated out of an earthly father's love, don't you?" the woman said kindly. "But God wants to fill that void in your life. God is our Father—your Daddy!" She reached for another tissue and handed it to me. "God's face lights up when you come to Him in prayer. You can climb up into His lap and tell Him everything. You are His special girl, Cathy."

Well, I tried to picture God like that, but it was hard. A barrier loomed between me and God, so I couldn't get close to Him. *What is it, God? I want to know You as my very own Father. I want to hear You say I'm Your very own special girl. Why can't I believe it?*

One day in class, I got a hint of what might be keeping me from a closer relationship with God. One of our teachers was speaking about bitterness. "When people hurt us, we put up walls," he said. "We think this will protect us from more hurt, but often the worst enemy is inside those walls. That enemy is bitterness. An unforgiving spirit ties us emotionally to the person who has hurt us. Bitterness hurts God. It breaks His heart. It is one of the sins that nailed Jesus to the cross. Unless we get rid of bitterness, it will poison us and all our relationships—including our relationship with God."

I knew he was talking about me.

That afternoon, I stayed behind after our small group prayer meeting to talk to our leader. "I know there's bitterness in my heart towards my dad," I said. "But what do I do about it?"

"Confess it to God, and ask Him to forgive you," she smiled. "Then ask your dad to forgive you."

"Ask my dad to forgive me? Shouldn't it be the other way around? I mean, he's the one who hurt me." I blurted out.

"Your dad's been hurt by your bitterness, Cathy," the woman said kindly. "You need to ask him to forgive you for that."

My cheeks were hot as I ran to my room. Grabbing my writing pad and pen, I hoisted myself to the top bunk. "*Dear Dad*," I began. Then my mind froze. The words wouldn't come. *It's not fair!* Hot anger welled up inside. *Dad should be the one apologizing to me.*

I jumped off the bunk and began to pace.

"What's up, Cathy?" my roommate asked.

"Oh, nothing," I yelled, as I fled out the door and down the steps. I'd go into the woods and work out. That always helped when I was upset.

An hour later, I knew what I would do: I would wait for my dad to write me first. He would ask me to forgive him. Then I'd say, "Oh, sure, Dad, I forgive you."

Next, I would ask him to forgive me. He'd say, "What for?"

And I'd say, "Bitterness, Dad." Then he would forgive me, and we would be friends again.

It made sense that it should happen this way.

But it didn't. Instead, as the days went by, my uneasiness grew. I kept hearing our teacher's words: "Bitterness is like a sliver. If left alone, it will fester and get worse and worse. It will poison you and all your relationships. You must release the hurt to Jesus. You must let Him pull out the sliver.

Confess your sin of bitterness to God and to the person who's hurt you. Only then can God heal you of the hurt."

One day, I couldn't stand it any longer. I knew if I didn't take care of bitterness soon, I would end up becoming a bitter person—like the ones I'd seen in the psychiatric hospital. If I continued hurting Jesus with my bitterness, God would never become real to me.

I grabbed my blue-checked stationery and began to write. Tears fell onto my page and smudged the words.

"Dear Dad," I began. *"I want to ask you to forgive me."* Then the words just tumbled out:

I've had resentment in my heart towards you, and I know I've hurt you. Dad, I love you. I have such sweet memories of you. I remember the times you helped me with my homework. You were so gentle and patient as I made the same mistakes again and again. I also remember the times we went canoeing and you kept encouraging me to go on or told me to rest when I needed to. You are such a loving father and so patient. But I haven't been patient with you. Please forgive me.

> *Dad, I love you so much.*
> *Cathy*

I had finished my letter. Then I thought of something else to say. I grabbed a piece of white scrap paper and scribbled: *"Dad, I haven't given up hope that you will be healed one day. The grace and mercy of God will heal you. Look up Psalm 147, verse 3. It's for you, Dad."*

Something happened to me that day while I was writing the letter. At the time I couldn't have explained it, but now, three years later, I think I can: it was like pulling the plug on a sink full of dirty water. Something unclean and ugly left me, and all I could think about was how much I loved my dad and how much I didn't want to hurt him any more. At the same time, the barrier between me and God had melted away, and I began to really feel God's love for me.

I had no idea how my dad would react to my letter. Would he even read it? Would he respond? During the following month I sometimes wondered, but it really didn't matter. I was free. As I prayed for him daily, sometimes the tears would fall, but now they were not tears of hurt but tears of love. I wanted Dad to be free and whole and happy again.

Exactly one month after I had written my letter, I pulled a blue airmail envelope out of my letter box. A letter from my dad! The scrawled address told me Dad's hands had shaken badly. Now, as I fumbled with the letter, I felt my heart race.

I plopped myself into the nearest chair, stuck a pencil into the corner flap, and flipped the envelope over. Right over the seam of the flap Dad had written in his scrawled handwriting, "*I love you! God loves you.*" Eagerly I ripped the letter open.

> *Dear Cathy,*
>
> *Thank you very much for your letter. It was so encouraging! God loves me and forgives me! I forgive you, dear, for everything. Please forgive me for being so callous, especially during your visits. I'm truly sorry.*
>
> *I love you very much and have happy memories of being with you. I am trusting God to make me well and take me home in due time. For a long time I did not pray or read the Bible. But God has forgiven me.*
>
> *Thank you for sending me the Swiss chocolate bar. I enjoyed it! I miss you, Cathy, and love you very much.*

I hope you can read this letter. The lithium medicine makes my hands shaky.

Love, your dad"

I bounded up the stairs to my room, two at a time. "A letter from my dad," I shouted to my roommates.

I read and reread that letter. Not only had my dad said those powerful words "I forgive you," but he'd asked me to forgive him. And his positive attitude surprised me. Was there a change in him?

When I had decided to let go of my bitterness towards my dad, I'd done it mostly for my own healing, but now it seemed as if healing were coming to my dad also. With God's love once more flowing between us, who could tell what wonderful things would happen next?

Editor's Note:

Cathy's dad has recovered sufficiently to be living in a group home. Cathy, and her brothers and sisters, keep in touch and visit him when possible.

Catherine Lescheid

The Power of Forgiveness[71]

I picked up the phone in the dormitory hallway. The moment I heard my father's voice, I knew he'd been drinking again. Without any greeting, he snapped, "You owe me money."

"What money?"

"Two hundred fifty dollars for car insurance."

When? My mind raced, trying to remember, as I fought a wave of panic. I'd been praying that my father and I would have a good relationship. Now, after not speaking to me for months, all he could say was, "You owe me money."

"I'll see what I can do," I stammered.

My father started swearing at me. "You're nothing but trouble."

"What have I ever done to you?" I choked. "I've prayed for you—"

"I don't want your prayers," he shouted. "You can leave us alone." Then his words became really vicious, "Change your last name; I don't want you to be part of my family."

Dazed, I hung up the receiver. I felt as if I'd been kicked in the stomach. I couldn't breathe. I went numb as the realization hit me: I'd been rejected by my father again. He didn't want anything to do with me.

I was thirteen years old when my mother told me I had been adopted. "Your biological father walked out when you were three months old and your sister was three years old."

She had married John Manzey, a tough, hard-working rancher, a year later. I had grown up with six siblings; Mom had two children and Dad had four children, two boys and two girls, when they married. Later, another sister was born. Life was hard in the South Dakotas, but Dad worked hard and made a good living. He was a good, church-going man, except when he drank. Then his temper flared out of control. And all too often, I was at the receiving end of it.

I grew up wondering why my father treated me differently than my older brothers. He'd buy them expensive boots and get me a cheap pair from Kmart. Once, I was driving a pickup behind my brother Brian's big truck on a dirt road on our ranch. Suddenly Brian stopped, and I stopped, too. He began to back up, but I couldn't get the pickup into reverse. Tom, sitting beside me, shouted for him to stop. But it was too late. Brian backed into the pickup. We climbed out of the pickup just as Dad's truck pulled up behind us. Dad jumped out, put his arm around Tom, and said, "It's okay. It wasn't your fault."

"I wasn't driving," Tom said, "Justin was."

Dad's face clouded as he turned towards me, "I've warned you over and over again," he shouted. "Can't you do anything right?"

When things like this happened, Mom felt bad for me. "Try to understand, Justin," she'd say. "Your father's having a hard time." She tried to compensate by cooking my favourite food or doing other things to please me. Her favouritism towards me infuriated my father even more.

One day, I was on the phone talking to a friend.

"Get off the phone," Dad hollered.

Before I had a chance to say goodbye, he shoved me aside and ripped the phone off the wall. "When I tell you to get off, I mean *now*!" he shouted.

I gave him a stone-cold stare. How I hated him.

Then hard times fell upon our family and my father lost everything—the ranch, all the horses, cattle, machinery, some vehicles, all his savings—and what wasn't lost was sold to try to survive. Feeling completely broken, my father had to start all over again with nothing.

My father went back to school to become an insurance broker, but he hated it. He hated the men who had robbed him of everything he'd worked for. Trying to cope, he drank even more. His behaviour grew more and more out of control.

Our family fell apart. Each of us boys handled the tension in our home differently. My brother Tom used drugs and alcohol; he broke into stores and stole cars. It became an ordinary occurrence to have the police at our house for a variety of reasons. My other brother and sisters all found ways to express their frustration. I vented my anger and bitterness in wrestling, kick-boxing, and fighting.

One day when my girlfriend and I were in the house, my father stormed at her, "Get out of my house." He grabbed my girlfriend's arm and shoved her toward the door.

"Don't touch her," I yelled.

My father pushed me onto the patio. "You get out, too," he shouted. "Don't ever come back." I went to my girlfriend's house to stay the night.

The next day when my father was away, I went back to our house to pick up my stuff. As usual, Mom wanted me to come back home. "Dad didn't mean it," she said. But I didn't trust him. I picked up my clothes and my Bible and headed back to my girlfriend's house.

My life out of control, I began to ask questions. "God, are You real? What's the truth? What's life about, anyway?" My friends and I would be drinking beer and reading the Bible, trying to find some answers.

When I was eighteen, I was a black belt instructor of a Tae Kwon Do school held at the fitness centre in Watertown, South Dakota. One day, my top instructor, who ran several schools, stopped in my office and asked his usual question, "How's it going, Justin?"

Normally, I'd tell him about my class, but this time I blurted out, "Man, I need Jesus."

My instructor stared at me. "What did you say?"

"Nothing," I said, feeling suddenly embarrassed. I started to swear.

"Justin, stop," he said. "You did say something." He studied my face earnestly. "You said you need Jesus."

"Yeah, I do," I stammered. I didn't know he was a Christian. I just knew I had to get my life together.

My instructor closed the office door. "Would you like to accept Jesus right now?"

I didn't know what he meant, but after he explained, I prayed, asking Jesus to forgive my sins and to come into my life. From then on, I began to think about what God wanted me to do with my life.

About a year later, I was driving my truck through town when I heard a Voice as clearly as though somebody had spoken out loud: "*You need to forgive your father.*"

"Never," I said.

Tears of rage blinded my eyes. I parked my truck in an empty parking lot. "I'll never forgive him," I shouted as I hit the steering wheel with my fist. "After what he's done, he doesn't deserve forgiveness." Bitterness choked me. "He's not even my father."

"*Then I can't forgive you.*"

Like a movie in slow motion, I saw what I had done wrong. Stuff I'd done before I became a Christian. One scene especially made me recoil. My brother Tom had come home in a drunken stupor and beat up my sister so badly that her face was unrecognizable. In a rage, I had seized him and beat him up until his eyes rolled back and he slumped to the ground.

"Oh, God, You have to forgive me," I moaned.

"I do forgive you, Justin."

Other scenes flashed before me: I saw, once more, each time my father had rejected me. As I felt the pain again, I started to cry.

"Forgive him," God's voice spoke gently. I began to see that unforgivingness was another form of rejection. Not only was I rejecting my father, but I was also rejecting God's offer to heal me of *my* past hurts.

"God, I want to be free of the pain of rejection," I prayed, "Please help me forgive him."

Then God showed me how His own heart was broken by my sin. I remembered words from Romans in the Bible, "God demonstrates His own love for us in this: While we were still sinners, Christ died for us."[72] God didn't wait for us to change before He offered His forgiveness. He took the first step. I knew He'd want me to forgive, even when the one who had hurt me didn't ask for it.

"God, this is so hard," I cried.

Eventually, I was able to say each time, "I forgive him for that," and really mean it.

Three hours later, I felt as if a huge weight had rolled off my shoulders, and in its place was peace. I felt clean, as if I'd had a deep, cleansing bath.

I wanted to tell my father and brothers what had happened.

But when I told my father, "I forgive you," he said, "What for?" He acted as though he'd never done anything to hurt me. For two years, I just prayed for my father and my family without seeing any results. My visits at home were as explosive as ever. Many mornings I'd wake up in a cold sweat after dreaming of my father's abuse.

Then one day, out of the blue, Tom called me. He and

his wife were smoking pot, and doing drugs, and using a Ouija board. "I hate my life," he said.

I drove over to his house, and the first thing I said was, "Tom, I forgive you."

Tom started to cry. We talked for a long time, and both he and his wife accepted the Lord. From then on, our relationship changed from one of hostility to one of deep respect.

Brian also responded positively when I said, "I forgive you," and God began to heal our relationship.

But nothing happened between my father and me. Even though I prayed every day for him, things got worse. And then the call came to the dorm when my father demanded I change my last name because he didn't want me in his family.

Some guys down the hall, realizing I was upset, came into my room. "What's wrong, Justin?" they asked, but I couldn't talk.

Then, one guy said, "God is telling me he needs money." He opened his wallet and put $50 on the table; another guy put $20 down; another, $100. Later when I counted it all up, it was $250, the exact amount I owed my father.

I stuffed the money into an envelope and reached for a piece of paper. I wanted to write my father a brief note, but my hand shook so badly, I couldn't write "Dad." I was about to seal the envelope without a note, but a Voice stopped me.

"Justin, forgive him."

"But God, I have forgiven him, and all he ever does is reject me."

"How often do I forgive you, Justin?" The Voice of Jesus was gentle, persistent.

"God, I want to forgive, but it's so hard," I cried.

I grabbed my pen and paper and stared at it. Suddenly, the words tumbled out:

"Dear Dad," I wrote, *"I'm praying for you. If ever you're in trouble, I'll be there for you."* Then I signed, *"Your son, Justin."*

My father did not reply.

Six months after I sent the letter, my sister called from home with bad news. Mom had called the cops to our house, and while they had stood beside my dad, she had delivered divorce papers. She left the state and didn't tell anybody where she was going. "Dad went crazy," my sister said. "He's been in a drunken stupor ever since."

"I'll call him," I said.

"Don't. He doesn't want to hear from you."

After I got off the phone with my sister, I called my father.

"Who's this?" He was cautious, and his speech was slurred.

"Your son, Justin," I said. Then, in a rush, I added, "Dad, I told you I would be there for you if ever you're in trouble."

My father was silent for a moment, then his words tumbled out: "I'm cursed," he said. "I've lost my wife…my family…my ranch…my insurance business…" He started to cry. "Nothing ever works out for me."

"Dad, I believe there's still hope."

"Tomorrow it will be over," he said wearily.

"What do you mean?"

"I'll drive my car over the bridge—"

"Dad, I'll send someone to help you."

"Nobody wants to help me."

"God wants to help you, Dad."

"I don't believe in God any more."

I had to get help to my father, but how? I called a friend who agreed to help. He got two other men to go with him, one man himself a recovered alcoholic. They visited my father and were able to persuade him to go with them to a rehabilitation centre.

During the months of therapy, my father gave up drinking. Eventually, he accepted the Lord Jesus as his own Saviour from sin. My mother accepted the Lord also. In time God healed their marriage, and they're together again. One night, I dreamed that my father was hugging me. I knew then that God's healing had reached a deep level in my heart. I don't fear my father any more.

Now when I return home, my father meets me at the airport. He gives me a warm embrace and, with tears in his eyes, he tells me, "I'm glad you've come home, Justin—my son." He tells me he's proud of me and he believes in what I'm doing.

Also, my brothers and sisters are eager to see me. We're not the same family any more. Forgiveness has opened the door for bitterness to leave and allowed God to come in and begin to restore our family. There are still times when we need to forgive one another. We're not a perfect family, just a family that has found the grace of God to forgive one another time and time again.

Justin Manzey

If you think you are suffering abuse by a parent or legal guardian, find a pastor or a counsellor and let him or her know of the situation. Perhaps all you need is counselling. If the abuse is more serious, contact an authority person you can trust and ask, "What do you think I should do?" Perhaps you need to contact social services or the police. Tell them, "I need help. I don't know what to do. Whom can I call?"

Gems of Truth: Let Go of Past Hurts

As God's chosen ones, holy and beloved…forgive each other;
just as the Lord has forgiven you, so you also must forgive
(Colossians 3:12,13 NRSV).

After I gave my life to God, I was still haunted by memories of the violence I had experienced at the hands of my father. I was a free-spirited teenager, eager to explore my world, but my father interpreted my behaviour as rebellion. When I wouldn't tow the line, he beat me, kicked me, pulled my hair, and knocked out my front teeth.

But I was twenty-two now, and the last beating had taken place six years ago. I was married and had two children of my own. I wanted to get on with my life; still, the nightmares of the past kept spinning in my head. Whenever I had a moment to contemplate life, I asked the questions: Why did he hurt me? Why did he beat me? Why? Why? Why? Six years of obsessing about past hurts kept me stuck in a cycle of bitterness and anger.

One day I was doing the laundry downstairs—all those stinky diapers a mother of babies has to do—and I thought how bitterness is like a stench that permeates all of life. We owned a Hoover washing machine with a mini washer on one side and a spinner on the other. The clothes were not properly balanced inside, and the machine kept spinning out of control. Spinning. And shaking. And knocking around the room. *Just like your mind,* I thought, *going around and around and around with painful flashbacks.*

I felt a gentle tugging on my heart. *"Trudy, it's been six years you've been rehashing your suffering. Don't you think it's time to let go?"* The Holy Spirit's gentle nudging continued. *"Remember the freedom you felt when first you grasped God's forgiveness? Let go of your father's wrongdoing. If you don't forgive him, God cannot forgive you,.*" The Spirit's words kept coming. "*You'll be spinning out of control like this crazy Hoover washer.*"

I knew God had spoken. I knelt down among the dirty clothes on the floor and prayed, "God, I find it so hard to forgive my dad. I know he'll never say 'sorry.'" I sniffled and wiped away the tears. "But I want to forgive him. I want to be free of this burden of bitterness. Give me the strength to let go of past hurts. I release my father now the best I know how."

What happened next is hard to describe. Jesus met me in an incredible way. Immediately I experienced an exhilarating peace. The bitterness and anger drained away, and in their place came a desire to know my father better.

As the years progressed and I forgave my father each time another memory surfaced, our relationship healed. Instead of the stench of bitterness, a sweetness began to permeate our relationship. It made me think of the saying: "Forgiveness is the perfume that the trampled flower casts back upon the foot that crushed it."

After my mother died, my father began to depend on me more and more.

When I look at him now—he playing harmonica and me accompanying him on the guitar—music fills my heart. In place of the grating, out-of-control noise of bitterness, God has given us the sweet harmony of forgiveness. Forgiveness has given me back my father.

Trudy Beyak

Father, I surrender my right to be hurt and hateful. I parcel up these bitter experiences and give them to You now. Take away the bitterness I feel toward the person who hurt me. Help me to truly forgive him or her as You have forgiven me.

Love Bridges the Gap[73]

I had just finished speaking to a Christian women's club in a town many miles from home. I was saying goodbye to the women at the door when my host, clearly agitated, arrived at the restaurant.

"Your son was on the phone. He and his wife are passing through town, and he wants to know if you'll meet them for lunch at the White Spot."

I was stunned. My son, who hadn't wanted to talk with me in three years, who had visited in my hometown and not let me know that he was there, now wanted to see me. "Where did he call from?" I asked. "When am I to meet them?"

"I don't know." You can be sure I left the restaurant in a hurry and waited by the telephone, hoping my son would call again to give me the particulars. He did, and we had a wonderful reunion. Not much was said, but both of us sensed that it was the beginning of healing a strained relationship.

In talking with women, I find many a mother's heart is broken because a son or a daughter is avoiding her. "My daughter's phone calls are brief and businesslike," says one. "My daughter has time for everyone else but me," says another.

I pass on to them what has helped me during such a difficult time. As in my case, often an estrangement develops during a traumatic time such as a death or a divorce. Raw emotions take time to process. We need to give our children time and space to sort it out. No amount of talking will help the situation. In fact, much talking makes it worse. It's like egg whites—the more you beat them, the bigger they get. We can't hurry up the healing process, in ourselves or in another person.

In the meantime, we can be grace givers. Grace lets another person be who they are, gives freedom to grow, to decide, to fail and to mature at his or her own rate. "Because you respect yourself, you allow your daughter [and son] the freedom to not live up to your expectations," writes Ingrid Trobisch.[74]

We can pray for our children and wait expectantly that Jesus, the great Reconciler, will bring us together again. And when He does, we can be there with a warm embrace.

Grace to Forgive

After a brief vacation, I was looking forward to going back to work as a registered nurse in a nursing care home. During seventeen years of happy service, I had forged strong friendships with staff and patients. So what happened that morning came as a total shock. Without any preamble, the director of nursing care told me, "You no longer have a job."

I was stunned.

And yet, in a sense, I'd seen it coming. For the past three years, I had felt pressure from the administration to retire, but I'd dismissed their not-so-gentle hints with a shrug. Didn't everybody past fifty-five get that? I loved my nursing job and my patients, and I intended to work another three years. When I felt ready to retire, I would say my goodbyes and gently close that chapter of my life and begin another one.

But the door had slammed shut involuntarily.

I felt it was so unfair! On my trips to town, I would speed past the once-friendly place and think, *I don't care if I ever set foot in that place again.* Immediately, a sadness would wash over me. *Do I want to finish a very rewarding nursing career with bitterness and resentment?*

No way! For the past weeks I had been learning about grace: how grace meets an unfair situation with forgiveness and goodwill. Here was my opportunity to practise what I had learned. But what could I do? Well, I could walk back into the nursing home and invite all the nursing staff—including the nursing director—to a potluck dinner at my home. At the very least, it would end my term of service in a more congenial way. You can be sure my heart pounded as I walked into the home to post my invitations, but I'm glad I did.

On the appointed day, sixteen people, each bringing a dish of delectable food, crowded into my small home. Soon the room resounded with laughter at good-natured nurses' jokes. As I looked into familiar faces and listened to the cheerful chatter, my heart warmed. In the many goodwill wishes I received that evening, I sensed a note of ongoing friendship.

My retirement from nursing didn't come the way I had envisioned, but truth is, it brought a blessing I might have missed: an opportunity to see the grace of Jesus at work in my nursing colleagues and in me.

The Symphony

My friend and I arrived early at the church for the performance of the Abbotsford symphony. "Shall we sit here?" she asked, stopping at a row of seats near the front.

I looked up and wanted to shout, "Not here, please." For in the very next row sat Susan,* my former head nurse, who had been responsible for my getting fired from a job.

"*You've decided to forgive her,*" a small Voice whispered. "*So why not sit here?*"

"She'll turn around, and I will have to speak to her," I argued back. Not wanting to make a scene in front of my friend, though, I sat down reluctantly.

But you can be sure I did not get the full benefit of the wonderful performance of the Abbotsford symphony. Other voices—discordant voices—clamoured for my attention: *What she did was downright mean. She deserves to be shunned.* After all, did I not have a right to resent her? And yet, I knew that forgiveness is like a very narrow gate leading to a garden where God dwells. If you want to enter it, you can't hang onto extra baggage like resentment and bitterness. You must give up your right to be hurt.

"I want to forgive, Jesus, but it's so hard. Please, help me."

During intermission, I watched Susan rise and reach for what I thought was a clipboard. *How typical,* I thought. Always looking for new ideas to improve the efficiency of her ward, super-organized Susan often carried a clipboard as she made careful notes and charts of everything.

I tapped her on the shoulder. "Susan, did you take your clipboard to the *symphony?*" I asked in mock horror.

"Not on your life," she shot back with a laugh.

For a few moments, we chatted amiably as forgiven people do, then Susan joined her friends.

Later as I settled in to enjoy the second half of the music, a warm glow filled my heart.

This is the only way to live, I thought. *Life is too short for keeping grudges and spoiling symphonies.*

Put Your Guilt to Rest[75]

Maria wiped her flushed face. Soon her husband would be coming home from work. Quickly she checked supper in the oven: roast beef and potatoes, almost done. Fresh green beans and cucumbers out of the garden would add the perfect touch.

She grabbed a large bowl. Before heading to the garden, she checked on her toddler asleep in the bedroom. Damp curls ringed a cherub face. Maria's heart swelled with pride. How she loved her little girl.

While she picked the beans and cucumbers, a neighbour called across the fence. They talked for awhile, then Maria excused herself. Back in the kitchen, she began to snap the beans. Suddenly, she heard a strange noise coming from just below the living room window. She hurried to investigate. Horror gripped her as she saw her darling child's body lying crumpled on the floor, the cord from the drapes around her neck. Her little face was purple.

Feverishly, Maria cut the rope. "Breathe, baby," she begged.

But neither she nor the medics could save the child. Her baby died.

Many years later, I met Maria, a woman bent with age, in a nursing home. She choked out her story to me, her nurse—but not only to me; her remorse spilled over onto any of the nursing staff who would listen to her. Again and again, she relived the horror. She blamed herself for her daughter's death, even though we tried to reassure her that it wasn't her fault.

Past experiences, not properly dealt with, can haunt us for the rest of our lives. Yet, it is possible to be free of past failures and unresolved guilt if we will but act upon Saint Paul's advice: "I'm focusing all my energies on this one thing: forgetting the past and looking forward to what lies ahead."[76]

FORGETTING THE PAST.

Is it possible to erase all memories of what happened? No! Paul never forgot past activities he was now ashamed of. Yet, the past did not have a stranglehold on him. He did not cling to it in senseless rehashing. Why? He had released the past to God. How can *we* do that?

1. Face up to your past wrongs and let Christ forgive you and clear you of all guilt.

It is not God's will that we be reminded of past sins that we have confessed to Him. Satan would want us to wallow in remorse, but God says, "If we confess our sins to Him, He is faithful and just to forgive us and to cleanse us from every wrong."[77]

Forgiveness is immediate upon a contrite confession. Christ's sacrifice on the cross paid the entire debt. Now God has written "cancelled" over our record of sins. Paul embraced this fact with joy. Likewise, we must accept Christ's gracious offer of forgiveness and begin to think and act like forgiven people.

To get a handle on God's forgiveness, I recite Bible verses that assure me of God's love and forgiveness, adding "I stand on this truth." Eventually, my mind accepts God's truth and begins to be at peace again.

2. Forgive yourself.

When a young friend became pregnant in high school, she was devastated. Her parents and her church forgave her.

She knew God had forgiven her, but she could not forgive herself. Why? "I was the good Christian girl who didn't get herself into trouble," she said. Wounded pride kept my friend from forgiving herself. Eventually, though, she was able to humble herself and to let go of her failure.

Maria illustrates a second reason why many of us find it hard to forgive ourselves. As many parents do, she laboured under unrealistic expectations: I ought to be able to prevent all harm to my children. Therefore she blamed herself for the death of her little girl.

When I'm tempted to be too hard on myself, I ask myself, "If this had happened to the woman down the street, how would I feel towards her?" Chances are, I'd try to look at it objectively. Take Maria, for instance. She didn't deliberately set out to harm her child. As parents, we do our absolute best with what we've been given. And still, being imperfect, we sometimes fail. That's the nature of being human.

LOOKING FORWARD TO WHAT LIES AHEAD.

Instead of hanging on to energy-sapping remorse, Paul used past failures as a powerful motivator to work for God in the present. "I strain to reach the end of the race and receive the prize for which God, through Christ Jesus, is calling us up to heaven."[78]

Paul majored on God's grace and forgiveness, not on his failures.

God is bigger than our failures. When we give our failures to Him, He will weave them into His perfect plan for our lives. My young friend, now happily married, has a special empathy for unwed teen mothers. After Chuck Colson's release from prison, he founded Prison Fellowship, an inter-

*Name has been changed

national ministry to prisoners in many countries of the world. "God used my greatest failure to bring about His greatest good," he writes. In my own life, also, God has used failures, my own and others, to bring about His good purposes.

Although we can't undo past failures, we can let go of guilt and remorse. We can turn our failures over to God and watch Him make something beautiful out of them. The choice is ours.

When I'm having a hard time letting go, I ask myself, "Do you want to be chained to that painful moment forever? Or do you want to claim your right to the divine grace God gives and be free of it?" I don't want to make the mistake Maria did. So I put my failures to rest in God's hands and use all my energy to live each day with enthusiasm and joy. What about you?

Prayer

In the morning, O LORD, you hear my voice;
in the morning I lay my requests before you
and wait in expectation.

PSALM 5:3

Do not pray for easy lives;
Pray to be stronger people.
Do not pray for tasks equal to your powers,
Pray for powers equal to your tasks!
Then the doing of your work shall be no miracle,
But you shall be a miracle.
Every day you shall wonder at yourself,
At the richness of life which has come to you
By the grace of God.

PHILIP BROOKS

Prayer is God's answer to our poverty, not a power we exercise to obtain an answer.

OSWALD CHAMBERS[79]

God answers prayer two ways: sometimes He gives an outright miracle, and sometimes He gives an inside-ourselves miracle. Prayer is more about relationship than about answers.

Why Can't I Believe?[80]

The teacher's face, at the discipleship training school in Lausanne, Switzerland, shone as he described God being the kind of parent whose eyes light up when He sees you coming, whose face breaks out in a big welcoming grin that says, "I'm sure glad you're My child. I'm so proud of you."

I caught my breath: *Is God really like that?* But immediately, another thought doused a flicker of hope. *Well, maybe for some, but not for me.* My own father's face didn't light up at my coming. In fact, the last time I'd gone to visit him in the psychiatric hospital, he'd paid no notice of me, even though I'd told him that I was going away for seven months. Mom tried to tell me that my father didn't really mean to reject me—that it was his illness—but I couldn't forget all the times in high school my father had missed my dramas, concerts, and soccer games.

No matter what Mom said, it *felt* like rejection. And it hurt. And no matter how hard I tried to tell myself that I didn't care what my father did, I did care. So now as I listened to the teacher talk on about God as our loving, attentive Father, I began to fidget. Did she have to remind me how much I was missing?

Oh, I knew about God being a God of love and that in some vague kind of way He loved me. Didn't He love everybody? But to delight in me? That He was glad to have me as His child was wishful thinking.

And yet, I wanted it to be true.

Some days later, I looked up my teacher. "I've forgiven my dad, and he's forgiven me for having bitterness towards him," I said. "But I still can't believe that God really likes me." I looked down at the floor. "I know you're going to tell me that God loves me," my words came tumbling out. "He loves the whole world, right? So He has to love me, but to be fond of me like you said—" I shook my head. "I wish I could feel that."

"Tell me about your own father," the teacher said softly.

All throughout my telling her about my father being too depressed to notice me, she kept handing me tissues. I just couldn't control my tears. When I finished, she said, "Cathy, because your earthly father was unable to give you the attention you craved, you have a hard time believing that your heavenly Father would be any different. But God is a perfect Parent, and His love for us is perfect, also. He never gets sick, or tired, or too busy to notice us."

"I wish I could believe that," I said.

"I think this will help." My teacher reached for her Bible, opened it to Romans 8:15, and began to read, "For you did not receive a spirit that makes you a slave again to fear, but you received the Spirit of sonship [or daughters]. And by him we cry, 'Abba, Father.'" She looked up and said softly, "*Abba* is the same as our word *Daddy*." Her brown eyes twinkled as she said, "God is a *perfect* daddy—for you too, Cathy."

Before I left to go back to my room in the dormitory, I promised her I would read that verse often, and no matter how I felt, I would say to myself, "These are God's words to me."

For several weeks I did that, but the words just didn't mean much. *Why can't I believe it?* I'd cry into my pillow at night. *If only God would show me in a small tangible way that He takes notice of me, then I would know He cares about me.*

One sunny day in early February, during a free after-noon, I left the Youth With A Mission base near Lausanne and headed down the hill to the bus stop. I was tired of wearing glasses, and I wanted to buy cleansing solution for my eye contacts. I caught the bus to Epalinges, a small village near Lausanne. When I arrived at the pharmacy, the door was locked. I'd forgotten the Swiss custom of closing the shops for two hours over lunch.

Oh well, I'll go exploring the countryside, I thought. I ambled down a country road, slid down the banks of a ravine, and entered a small forest. At an exercise station, I put down my backpack and began to work out. Then I waded into a small creek and sat down on a flat rock. I pulled my Bible from my backpack and read my verse several times. After a while I felt chilly and decided to walk again. I crossed a small forest on the other side of the stream, then walked across a playground to a metro station, crossed it, and walked up a hill. At a quaint church I sat down on an old bench. Two hours later, I arrived at the pharmacy, bought the solution, and took the bus home.

It was almost dark as I got off the bus and walked up the steep hill towards the dorm. Supper would be in half an hour. I hurried to my room, put the backpack on the chair, and fished for the small round case that held my contacts. I couldn't find it. I turned the bag upside down and gave it a violent shake. Nothing.

"Great. I've got cleansing solution but no contacts," I mumbled to my roommate.

"Where did you lose them?" she asked.

"Who knows?"

When I told her where I'd been that afternoon, she looked worried. Finding my contact case in that maze would be like searching for a needle in a haystack.

Yet the next day, during our small group prayer time, it was my roommate who suggested we pray that I would find my contacts again.

"We've been learning about God being better than the best dad in the world," a boy piped up. "I think He cares about Cathy's contacts."

As I listened to the earnest prayers of my friends, I remained skeptical. Maybe God *could* find my contact case, but *would* He? After all, didn't He have better things to do?

The next morning, a friend offered to drive me back to the pharmacy. "Show me where you walked," he said. So I took him down the country road, through the forest to the workout station, and to the creek. He waded to the rock where I had sat the day before and peered into the water. I wanted to laugh. How in the world would he find a small contact case in that rushing stream? But my friend persisted in his search. We walked down the path to the busy playground. *Some child probably took it home,* I thought. At the metro station, people scurried across the platform to catch their subway. *Somebody probably kicked it into the bushes.* At the church, we checked all around the bench where I'd sat. Then my friend suggested we walk inside the church.

"But I wasn't inside the church," I protested.

"Somebody may have found it and taken it there," he said.

As time went on, I began to feel guilty. I was wasting my friend's time. "Let's call it off," I said. "I've still got my glasses, so I'm not really stuck."

Reluctantly, my friend got back into the van. I hopped in, and we headed back up the hill towards the school. *It's okay,* I told myself. *I knew all along that God wouldn't bother. He's got bigger things to worry about.*

We were almost back at the dormitory when I glanced

out of the window and saw something round and beige and familiar lying beside the road.

"Stop!" I yelled.

I hopped out and hurried back a few steps. Sure enough, it was my contact case. Had it been an inch closer to the road, it would have been crushed by cars driving over it. Had it been an inch closer to the side of the road, it would have been hidden by tall grass.

As I cradled the small object in my hands, joy flooded me. God really *did* care about me! He had helped me find my contact case, even when I didn't believe, even when it wasn't an absolute necessity. He wanted me to know that He cared—really cared—about me, so He'd shown me in a way I could understand.

"God, you really are my daddy," I whispered.

Catherine Lescheid

From the Brink of Hell

Peter Harper* picked up his son at the Vancouver International Airport and ordered him to get into his car. "We're going to the police station," he told his thirteen-year-old son.

As the car sped away, Andrew slouched beside his father. Neither of them spoke a word.

When they entered the police station, an officer was waiting for them. He lectured Andrew about the gravity of his crime: he and his buddies had stolen a car and driven it across the Rocky Mountains to Calgary, Alberta. On the second day there, the police had apprehended them and placed them on an airplane for home.

"It won't happen again," his father promised the officer.

At home his father ordered him to go to the bedroom. "I'll call you after your mother and I have decided what to do with you," he said. Andrew looked briefly at his mother, sitting dejectedly on a kitchen chair, her eyes red and swollen from crying.

I'm nothing but grief to my parents, he thought. *It's best I leave and never come back.* He looked around the bedroom. He had to get away before his father came back. Hurriedly, he took some money from the bedroom closet, raised the window in the ensuite bathroom, and pushed his body through. He dropped to the ground below, and, with just the clothes on his back, he ran away again. His foot-

*All names have been changed.

prints in the snow were all his parents saw of him for a very long time.

Andrew came from a good Christian home and had been raised in church. Still, he was a deeply troubled young man. Someone outside of his family home had abused him, but he felt he couldn't tell anyone. It would be tattling. Besides, nobody would believe him anyway. They might even blame him for it. So he locked the painful incident away to fester into rebellion. He started running with the wrong crowd and abusing drugs and alcohol. After his escape from home, Andrew lived on the streets with other street kids.

Ten years later his daughter, Erin, was born. Andrew tried hard to be a good father and family man. His family, seeing the change in him, thanked God for answering their prayers. But within a year, Andrew had walked out on his daughter and her mother. He cut himself off from all family contact again and returned to the street life. Still, his family never stopped praying for him.

One fateful day, Andrew borrowed a needle from another addict. The needle was contaminated with the HIV virus. Five years later, he developed full-blown AIDS. His weight plummeted from 250 pounds to 130 pounds. Too weak to walk, he used a cane, then a wheelchair. Finally he was hospitalized for eleven weeks. Still not speaking to his family, he was all alone when the doctor told him he would not live until Christmas.

Cindy, a hospital employee, noticed that the young man in Room 203 received no guests. Even the nurses did not spend much time with an AIDS patient. *Nobody deserves to be alone like that,* she thought. During lunch break one day, Cindy and Andrew met in an elevator going down. Andrew was on his way outside for a smoke.

"May I join you?" Cindy asked. "It's my lunch break."

As they sat in the shade of a cedar tree, Cindy asked, "So what's it like being on drugs and living on the street?"

Andrew found her blunt question amusing. But sensing a deep sincerity, he spoke to her frankly. His candour encouraged Cindy to confide in him about some events in her unhappy life. As they continued to meet on lunch breaks, they became good friends.

After Andrew was released from hospital, Cindy continued to visit him. One day she found him in a stupor, his mind crazed with morphine and alcohol. She struggled to put him into her car and drove him to a walk-in clinic. But by the time they got there, Andrew had lapsed into unconsciousness. "He will probably die before morning," the doctor said.

Cindy was shocked. There wasn't a hospital bed available, the doctor explained; she would have to take him home again. Home to his small room to die alone? No, she couldn't do that. She would take him to her apartment, she decided, and put him into her own bed.

To her immense relief, Andrew survived the night. But the next five days were a nightmare. It was difficult to know how to help Andrew, in the throes of withdrawal symptoms. Day and night, Cindy stood by his side, talking soothingly to him, encouraging him. Sometimes she could barely conceal her own fear and misgivings.

On the fifth day, his mind cleared. "What day is it?" he asked.

"Sunday, September 8," Cindy responded.

"Isn't this the day of the Christian concert?"

Cindy couldn't believe her friend remembered an invitation given several weeks before, and which he had tossed into the garbage can.

"You want to go?" she asked.

"If you'll go with me," he said.

Cindy drove to the stadium where Jaci Velasquez, a Christian contemporary artist, was performing. About halfway through the concert, Cindy noticed that Andrew began to fidget. *We should go home*, she thought.

Just then Jaci announced, "I'm going to dedicate the next song to my friend and her baby. Both of them have AIDS."

Andrew started as though she'd spoken directly to him. Had God singled him out? Was God calling him? "Let's go," he whispered to Cindy.

They left the stadium and headed for home. But Andrew couldn't shake the impression that God was pursuing him. When they passed a church, he told Cindy to drive into the parking lot and stop the car. "I've got to go inside," he said.

As they walked through the main entrance of the church, they heard singing and clapping. Steadying himself with a cane, Andrew walked down the centre aisle of the sanctuary past row upon crowded row to the front bench, with Cindy following right behind him. They sat down just as the song ended. A man left his seat on the platform and walked over to the couple. "I believe God wants me to talk to you," he said. "What can I do for you?"

"I want to get right with God," Andrew blurted out. "I've been running from Him for a very long time." On that day, in that small church, the prayers of Andrew's parents and family began to be answered as he surrendered his life to Christ.

In time Andrew was reconciled with his parents and his siblings. He asked his brother who was a pastor to baptize him. Then he phoned his parents, living on another continent, asking for their forgiveness. "Your mother and I are thrilled with the step you have taken," his father responded. "Just keep trusting the Lord."

There was one more bridge Andrew longed to cross. He wanted to be reunited with his eleven-year-old daughter, Erin. Would she want to reconnect with him? After all, he had walked out on her when she was one year old. Would she forgive him? To his immense relief, she did want to see her father again.

Andrew took a bus to the city where his daughter lived and checked himself into a hotel. He paced the hotel lobby, waiting for his daughter to arrive. What would she look like? What would they talk about?

Finally a young girl entered and hurried toward him. As she flashed him a warm smile, she said, "Hi, Dad!"

Erin sat down beside her father and showed him photographs of herself during the stages in life he had missed: a toddler with a fist full of dandelions, a kindergartner flashing a toothless grin, a girl in shorts showing off a ribbon won at a sport's event. She chatted happily to her father as though there had never been a separation. Ever since Erin had been four, she had prayed for her father, she told him. And now, as she leaned on his shoulder, her fervent prayers were answered.

The more inner healing Andrew experienced, the more physical healing he received. With medication his strength returned and soon his stature resembled that of a football player.

Cindy and Andrew were married. Working at a rescue mission, they bring hope to marginalized people who feel unworthy of love. Andrew tells them that there is no pit so deep that God's love isn't deeper still. "He brought me back from the brink of hell."

Mark's Miracle[81]

When Mark Frew, a civil engineer from Victoria, British Columbia, Canada, took his wife Debbie and their small son Jonathan to visit his parents in Zambia, it was a dream come true. Who could have known that it would turn into their worst nightmare?

After a delightful three-day Christmas celebration with family and friends, Mark left the Chizela Bible School compound where his parents were teaching and cycled through the bush to a newly planted soybean field to shoot pigeons. He put down his bike and began walking through eighteen-inch grass. Keeping his pellet gun ready, he looked up at the trees, stalking the birds. Suddenly he felt a sharp pain in his right foot. Mark jumped forward, then swung around, but he couldn't see the snake that bit him. No movement in the grass either. Still, it must have been a poisonous snake, for immediate cramping and swelling of his leg set in. Just above his tennis shoe on the back of his ankle, he saw two distinct puncture marks, one the size of a half-inch tear. He hollered for help and ran towards two boys working in the field. Just as the boys reached him, he collapsed. They immediately jumped onto Mark's bike and took off at high speed to get help. Mark ripped off his shirt and wound a tourniquet around his leg. Then he lay very still to slow down circulation.

What chance did he have? Chizela was 160 kilometres from the nearest mission hospital. Their only link with the outside world was radio call-up once a day, at 5:30 in the afternoon. He felt the paralysis creeping up his leg. *With some snakes, I could be dead in twenty minutes.* He shivered. *If I die, what will happen to Debbie and baby Jonathan? Lord, save me!*

Mark's father Keith jumped into his truck and raced down the dirt road towards the soybean field. Back at the station, he laid his son on the grass beside their house and began to suck on the wound. If only his wife Cindy and nurse Roxanne were here. They might know what else to do, but they were off in the woods searching for the flame lily that bloomed only once a year—at Christmastime. He checked his watch, 5:00 p.m., another half-hour before radio call-up. *That might be too late*, he groaned.

When the nurse arrived, she administered a shot of adrenaline and began a saline drip. She had no antivenom. Listening to Mark's anguished screams, she wished she had a strong painkiller to give him, but she didn't have any. He was vomiting violently. His leg swelled to the size of a large stovepipe. She monitored his vital signs. Still stable.

Keith hurried into the house and turned on the short-wave radio. He shouted above the static, "Chizela calling Mukinge. Do you read me?"

"You're coming through." Dr. Jim Foulkes' reassuring voice came from Mukinge Hospital. Twenty-six years ago, he had brought Mark into the world. He'd do anything now to help him.

"What snake bit Mark?"

Keith didn't know.

Dr. Jim scoured the hospital fridge for polyvalent pooled antivenom that counteracts a wide range of snake venoms, but he found none. He grabbed a vial of black mamba antivenom—it might do some good—and a few other emergency items and ran towards the airplane.

The fact that the airplane was home and ready to go was itself a miracle. Don Amborski, the pilot, had taken a group of men hunting for the day. They had planned to be gone until 9 p.m., but, the hunting not being good, they had decided to come home early. Don had just finished gassing up his ancient Cessna 185 when Dr. Jim called.

Thirty minutes later, Dr. Jim ran to Mark's side and administered black mamba antivenom and injected 100 CC's of normal saline into the bite site, hoping it would dilute the toxic effect of the venom. During the night, he also gave his patient a strong painkiller and penicillin.

A kerosene lantern suspended from a nail on the wall cast its meagre light on Mark's bed. He tried hard to focus on Debbie sitting beside his bed, but his vision was blurred. The paralysis was creeping up his stomach and into his chest cavity, making breathing difficult. Mark was still vomiting. "My leg's on fire," he screamed in pain.

Debbie held her husband's hand and mopped his forehead. "Don't leave us, Mark," she coaxed. "Try to hang on for us." For the sake of his wife and son, he forced himself to stay conscious, but he kept losing sight of her and her voice kept fading away.

Early streaks of daylight infused new optimism into the small group keeping vigil by Mark's bedside. Since his patient had survived the night, Dr. Jim concluded it must have been a puff adder that bit Mark. Prognosis of a full recovery was good. Even so, he wanted Mark in Mukinge Hospital, where he could monitor him closely. Don Amborski removed two seats from his airplane, and Keith carried his son to the plane and bedded him down. Debbie and Jonathan accompanied Mark, while Keith and Cindy drove their car to Mukinge Hospital.

At the hospital, Mark's leg was put into a sling and suspended from the ceiling. The puncture marks were still bleeding. To boost his platelet count, several blood transfusions were given, along with pooled antivenom, which a nurse found in a private fridge. Mark improved dramatically and began to play with his infant son. "I'll soon be home in Chizela," he teased.

But the following day, Mark started to hallucinate again. His face was dusky, and he was coughing. Fluid was detected in one lung, and his kidneys were failing. Blood was still oozing from his wounds. His ankle had turned black. He was in extreme shock.

If Mark could be sent to Johannesburg, he might have a chance, Dr. Jim thought. He dialled the Medical Rescue International Team for an air ambulance, but the phone was dead. "Oh God, show us a way to get through," he prayed.

It could take up to two days to make an international connection, far too late to be of any help. Frantically he dialled another agency, and after a few rings, a person answered. "I shall contact the MRI immediately," a woman said, "but you will need to put down a deposit of $10,000 U.S." Dr. Jim cringed. How was he going to collect that much money in such a short time?

But once more the impossible happened: the money was found and a deposit made. By the time Mark was transferred into the MRI air ambulance, he was unconscious. Debbie, Jonathan, and Cindy accompanied him on the one-hour flight to Johannesburg. Keith returned to Chizela Bible School to resume his duties there. He knew the entire church and student body were praying for them and would welcome an update.

At the Garden City Clinic in Johannesburg, a specialist gave a grim prognosis. "Mark has severe septicemia, pneumonia, kidney failure, and a serious blood clotting problem," he said. "We'll do what we can, but his chances of survival are slim." Immediately, Mark received more blood and aggressive antibiotic treatment. Still his fever raged out of control, and he kept hallucinating. The doctor made two incisions from his toes to his knee on both sides of his right leg to remove pus and dead tissue.

Meanwhile, at Chizela Bible School compound, many people kept praying earnestly.

One afternoon when Debbie and Cindy arrived at the hospital, they found Mark sitting up and smiling. For the first time in eight days, he had no pain, he said. Moreover, his temperature was normal and his colour was good. After several more operations to remove dead tissue, the long incisions on both sides of his right leg were closed with sutures and skin grafts.

After more than three weeks in hospital, Mark was discharged.

Mark and Debbie returned to Chizela to thank their many friends who had prayed for his recovery. As they exited the airplane, a group of Zambian women in colourful print dresses and head scarves pushed forward and encircled the family. They burst into song and dance and, with uplifted hands, praised God for His mighty power. For three weeks, people visited with Mark and Debbie—some coming from over twenty kilometres away—to take part in joyous thanksgiving. Their friend, who'd been as good as dead, had been raised to life again.

Editor's Note:

Mark was bitten by a Gaboon viper, an extremely rare occurrence in Zambia and almost always fatal. After a Gaboon viper strikes its victim, its short, fat body lies perfectly still in the grass. For this reason, Mark did not see nor hear the snake. In Canada, Mark received more surgery, intensive physiotherapy, and magnetic therapy. Today, he has fully recovered. He is back working for the department of highways, jogging and playing squash several times a week.

When You No Longer
Hear the Music[82]

*Born profoundly deaf, Glen Cuthbertson defied the odds,
learned to play the piano, and became an accomplished
concert pianist. Imagine not being able to hear without two
hearing aids, not even a single note of a powerful concert
grand piano. Imagine also that you're playing your most
difficult piece during a solo concert in a prestigious church
and your hearing aids suddenly go dead...*

Wearing a black tuxedo, I adjusted my position on the piano bench, breathed a quick prayer, and began to play my crowning piece, "The Battle Hymn Of The Republic." As my fingers flew over the keyboard, the music swelled to a glorious crescendo. In my mind's eye, I could see Jesus, the King, riding a white horse and bursting through the clouds to reclaim His people.

Abruptly, the sound faded away. Even though my fingers kept racing over the keys, I could not hear a single note. Both of my hearing aids had gone dead! "Oh God, help me," I groaned. Sweat beading on my forehead, I continued to play.

After I finished, I bowed and acknowledged the gracious applause. Then I turned around, inserted new batteries into my hearing aids, and finished the concert.

On the way home, my wife Ildiko and I laughed at this mishap. We had not the slightest inkling that my greatest test of faith lay just ahead.

As long as I can remember, sound and rhythm have fascinated me. While my father played the piano, I would crouch underneath the keyboard, straining to hear a muffled sound. Other times I would climb onto the piano bench and bang out my own "music." My mother would come running to stop the racket. When my parents discovered that I had been born profoundly deaf, they were deeply dismayed.

My first hearing aids were clumsy things with a long wire attached to them. But I was a good-natured two-year-old and left them in place. Seeing my delight with music, my parents enrolled me in piano lessons. Perhaps they thought it would keep me off the streets—and they were right. I practised many hours each day. After ten years, all my hard work paid off: I passed the Royal Conservatory of Music of Toronto grade eight piano with first class honours.

During my early teens, inspired by Dino Kartsonakis' music, I prayed, "Jesus, I want my music to touch people's lives. I give You my talent to use as You wish." Like the nameless boy in the Bible who gave his lunch to Jesus, I wanted Jesus to bless my talent and use it for His glory.

A year after our marriage, Ildiko encouraged me to follow my heart and make music my career. "But what if I can't support ourselves, and our future children?" I worried.

"God's anointing is on your music," she said. "I'll continue working until you can earn enough for us all."

I quit my job in a window and door shop, and in 1990, we launched our music ministry. But in the years that followed, bookings for concerts were slow. My income didn't nearly match the needs of our growing family with three small children. Yet, believing that God had called us to serve Him in a music ministry, we persevered.

At a church in Vancouver, British Columbia, Canada, I gave several concerts on a 1915 Steinway concert grand piano. The black finish, checkered with cracks, was dull and lifeless, and the keys, having lost their smooth responsiveness, resisted me. Yet the clear, pure sound sent shivers down my back. *I wonder if they'll sell it to me,* I thought. The pastor told me that many buyers had been turned down, even those who offered large sums of money. Well, I did not have any money, but I had faith that kept me dreaming about the Steinway and how I would fix it to be as good as new.

And then something happened that stretched my faith almost to the breaking point.

As I was tuning a piano in November 1994, I noticed that the notes sounded tinny. The sound stunned me, and I felt dizzy. Soon I couldn't hear anything in my right ear. *Must be because I'm stuffed up with a cold,* I thought. But a week later, the notes still sounded lifeless and flat. What's more, a sound roared in my head like a couple of Harley Davidson motorcycles racing by. The clamour—day and night, week after week, month after month—drove me crazy.

Doctors did their best to help me. "I suspect further auditory nerve damage," the specialist said. "It may signal the end of your hearing in the right ear altogether." My heart froze. *How can I be a musician if I can't hear?*

"Try to live with the noise the best way you can."

"But it's driving me crazy."

"To stop the noise, we could destroy the auditory nerve, but then your chances of ever hearing again in the right ear are gone. We don't recommend this. You're still young—"

As hard as it was to put up with the twenty-four-hours-a-day roaring in my head, I had to keep clinging to hope. I had to keep going on with my concerts. But how?

In the midst of this dilemma, a wonderful thing happened. The Vancouver church agreed to let me have the Steinway in trade for my Yamaha C7. The day the moving van brought home the coveted concert grand, I should have been jubilant. But a battle waged in my soul.

Is this some kind of mockery? my mind screamed. *God gives me my dream piano only to take away the ability to truly hear it. Lord, I've given You my talent, and I want to play for Your glory. Why are You doing this to me?*

Although I was angry with God, I kept clinging to Him and begging for a healing.

"God, please restore my hearing."

"*My grace is sufficient for you.*"

"How can I be a good pianist when I can't hear the music?"

"*My grace is sufficient for you.*"

"This noise is driving me crazy. Please, God, You have the power to stop it."

"*My grace is sufficient for you.*"

In desperation, I threw myself into rebuilding the Steinway. I worked ten hours a day, five days a week, for ten weeks. On weekends, with a friend helping me, we put in twice the hours. I repaired, restored, and cleaned as many of the original parts as I could, and those that were too badly worn, I replaced. Then I regulated the mechanical parts into exact tolerance. Finally, I refinished the piano to a brilliant lustre. I didn't know if I would ever be able to hear this magnificent concert grand piano again. Still, I couldn't leave it alone. Fixing up the Steinway was a labour of love that kept my mind off the constant roaring in my head.

As opportunities came, I continued to give concerts. As I played, I strained to hear the rich tones of my orchestral arrangements of "Our Father" or "The Battle Hymn," but I couldn't. Every piece seemed dull and lifeless to me. Yet to my surprise, people kept responding with encouraging notes to let me know my music had touched their hearts.

"We loved your concert and testimony and wept all the way home."

"My grandfather listened to your tape over and over. It gave him comfort in his last days."

"I was profoundly struck by how the dear Lord has woven you, your piano, and your message into perfect harmony. Thank you for the moment God called you and you said *yes.*"

As hard as it was, I had to keep going.

While on a concert tour in Ontario in 1998, I began to read Chuck Colson's book *The Body*. In it, he describes a Nazi concentration camp where ten condemned men await their execution. A priest encourages them to keep faith in Jesus Christ, even in the face of intense suffering and death. Then the priest takes the place of one of the condemned men and goes to his own death with dignity and courage.

As I read, I was deeply moved. What if I were facing my own death? Would it be so important that I could hear? Would I care so deeply about being a success as a musician?

"God, I want to be faithful to the end," I choked. "Help me to pay the price." I brushed away the tears that spilled onto my cheeks. "I relinquish my desire for healing," I whispered. "I'll give You my best, even if I never get my hearing back. Help me to carry on."

I still didn't like the constant roaring in my head, nor the fact that I could not hear, but I had more peace. Whatever God wanted was okay by me.

A month later, after a shower, I thought I heard the squish of water in my right ear. Then, while blow-drying my hair, I not only felt but heard the wind. *Don't get too excited*, I told myself. I had been obsessed with the desire for healing, and I didn't want to fall into that trap again. Then, to my utter relief, the noise in my head stopped.

Ildiko was ecstatic. "Maybe God will restore your hearing after all," she said. A timid hope grew with the weeks as my right ear began to pick up more distinct sound.

One day, with my hearing aids in place, I sat down in front of the gleaming Steinway and put my hands on the keys. As I played my rendition of "Our Father," an indescribable beauty came to my ears. For the first time in over two years, I could clearly hear the high notes. They sparkled like diamonds in a darkened sky. The song took on form as I had imagined it all those years I couldn't hear. The music pushed through my fingers and pulsated into the room. My spine tingled with excitement. My heart almost burst with praise to my Father: what an awesome God!

Now when I play "The Battle Hymn" during a concert, I visualize Jesus, the King, coming through the clouds. But also I see Him as a compassionate Saviour who touched my ears so I could hear again. It was when I relinquished what I thought I needed and said *yes* to God that He gave me back my heart's desire.

Glen Cuthbertson

Abundant Grace⁸³

I t's time to go on a ventilator," the doctor said. He might as well have been pronouncing my death sentence. Not that I was afraid of new challenges—God knows, in my forty-two-year fight with muscular dystrophy, I had conquered dozens of obstacles. But a ventilator? I wasn't about to give up my independence to a noisy breathing machine.

"No, thanks," I told the doctor. I would continue to row my boat like mad, and God would provide the favourable current. That's how I'd managed my life so far.

From the age of three, I had tripped over my feet and fallen, picked myself up and fallen again, more often than I could count. One winter afternoon, on my way home from junior high school, I kept falling in the snow. With enormous effort, I struggled to my feet and staggered home. I could have frozen to death, but my desire to live a normal life kept me out of a wheelchair until I reached age eighteen.

Even with the wheelchair, I determined to keep my independence. I devised a platform with pulleys that my grandfather and uncle built for me. My "elevator" enabled me to leave the house on my own so I could take part in school and church functions.

At twenty-five, I married Margaret. We knew life would not be easy, but we loved each other. Besides, we believed God wanted us to walk this road together. Beyond the limitations of the wheelchair, we expected life to be normal.

Margaret began to teach elementary school. I graduated from the university with two master's degrees. Eventually I landed a good job as a testing expert in the medical school at the University of Washington. We bought a home in Seattle. Our teen girls, Erin and Allison, enjoyed life. I prided myself in what we were able to accomplish despite my handicap. We lived a bit closer to the edge of life, perhaps, but we faced the same joys, the same hurts, as any average American family. I wasn't about to change that.

Then one hot mid-August night, I awoke at 4 a.m. feeling short of air. I woke up Margaret, and together we made it through a very long, miserable night. In the morning, when sitting up, I could breathe better. "Probably indigestion," I said. But the next night, the same thing happened. For the next six weeks, my air hunger increased. Finally, in October, we went to the doctor. *He'll give me some pills to clear this up,* I thought. Instead, he told us the worst possible news: I needed a ventilator.

The idea of being hooked up to a noisy machine twenty-four hours a day repulsed me. I'd be a nuisance in public places. I might as well say goodbye to church functions, the theatre, and symphonies. And vacations in Sun River with my family? Forget that. No, we'd find a way to conquer this new challenge without surgery.

Margaret and I struggled on, month after weary month. With a pneumo belt, I was still able to work at the university, but often I fell asleep. When I couldn't concentrate any more or carry on a normal conversation, I resigned from my job. At home, I spent twenty-four hours each day sitting in a wheelchair. I had lots of time to brood. Where was God in all this? Why wasn't He helping us?

Nights were the worst. Gasping for air, I'd wake up Margaret to help me change my position. One night, her nerves snapped. She wailed, a piercing cry of agony that woke up our girls. Alarmed, they bolted downstairs. The terror in my children's eyes and the agony on my wife's face shocked me. *What am I doing to my family?* That night I decided to lay down my pride: I would have the surgery.

After the emergency throat surgery, a ventilator, with tubing almost as big as the hose on a vacuum cleaner, was hooked up to the plastic tube in the slit in my throat. The nurse turned on the machine, and a noisy swish forced 1,200 CC's of air into my lungs. Nurses and specialists worked around the clock to make life tolerable for me. People from church dropped in with cards, flowers, and promises to pray. In time, I learned to swallow again and to speak. "Hi, beautiful," I said to my wife. She answered with a radiant smile.

Six weeks later, the respiratory therapist handed Margaret a manual. "Read this," he said. "You'll need to know what to do when Fred comes home." As she reached for the manual, I read the panic in my wife's eyes. In a flash, I remembered a night torn by a piercing wail of agony and saw again the horror on my children's faces. And in remembering, guilt washed over me. *By choosing to live, have I sentenced my family to a life of misery?*

Day after day, I brooded over what I now considered a selfish decision. *Margaret deserves better than to be saddled with a disabled person like me.* Had I opted for no medical intervention, I would have died. My death would have set her free to live a full and normal life. Not only had I lost my independence, but I had become a burden to my loved ones. I had nothing left to give, and a life of always taking from others was worse than meaningless.

When people dropped by to say they were praying for us, I would think, *God has done all He's going to do for me. It's time for God to move on to the next guy.*

Yet their continued prayers unleashed a silent power. Like relentless sunbeams, they pierced through my black despair.

One morning, I began to notice the upbeat comments of the nurses. Astonished, I listened as they discussed a workable home care plan for my wife and me. Most of all, I heard the ring in my wife's voice as she said, "I'm glad you chose to live, Fred."

I began to glimpse a new insight into God's mysterious working: for those who can still paddle, God provides a favourable current, but for those of us who can't paddle any more, He Himself becomes the current, as the Scriptures say, "Christ in you, the hope of glory."[84]

On the day of my discharge, ten years ago, the sun stood at high noon. I drove my chair, with the ventilator behind me, into our backyard filled with people cheering a welcome. A huge banner spanned the sky: Welcome Home, Fred! Balloons of all colours fluttered from trees. I revelled in every bit of colour, every picture on the wall, every sound and smell of home.

Two months after I returned home, I went back to work at the University of Washington.

All these years, my wife has worked alongside me as a program coordinator. Two nurses, on a rotating basis, attend to my needs at night. No denying it, life has been hard. The years have been a mixture of triumph and joy, carved out of much agony. But to see both daughters graduate, from high school and college, to help teach the girls to drive, to celebrate our twenty-ninth wedding anniversary, to attend church and live theatre again, to go biking and wheel chairing with my family in Oregon's beautiful Sun River—these are not ordinary events. They're God's extravagant grace-gifts to me.

I struggled long and hard to be self-reliant, but it was only after I traded in self-reliance for God-reliance that I discovered God's mighty power.

Fred Shannon

Editor's Note:
Fred Shannon died in July 1996 after being married to Margaret for thirty years.

One Faithful God—
Two Different Prayer Answers[85]

Sandy and I attended the same small group Bible Study at church. During a time of sharing prayer requests, we often requested prayer for our husbands, who were ill.

Sandy's husband suffered from kidney failure. Despite dialysis, his health was deteriorating rapidly. He desperately needed a kidney transplant, but in four long years no suitable donor was found. Her husband was becoming so ill that if he didn't get a transplant soon, he would die.

My husband was hospitalized with severe depression. Despite the latest and best treatments, he was getting worse. He attempted suicide several times and threatened to kill his family. Over the years, new drugs were tried and more therapy sessions followed, to no avail. "There isn't much more we can try," the psychiatrist said. "Your husband is chronic."

I asked the group to pray for a miracle. "God can do the impossible," I said.

As the group prayed earnestly, Sandy and I found consolation in hearing our needs brought to God again and again. "We're the most prayed-over people in the group; something is bound to happen," we told each other.

And it did. One day, Sandy could barely express her joy as she told the group of a late phone call one night. A donor had been found, and arrangements had been hurriedly made for her husband to be admitted to hospital. There was great rejoicing in the group that evening and more earnest prayer that the transplant would be successful. A month later,

Sandy's husband was at home recuperating. Soon he was back at work. God had indeed answered prayer and brought about a miraculous healing.

Meanwhile, my husband returned home also but was soon hospitalized again. Raised hopes followed dashed hopes, year after year. Psychiatrists, baffled by the situation, kept changing the diagnosis: clinical depression, early Alzheimer's, manic depressive disorder, then dementia. He was moved to a care home. The stress of the years wreaked havoc in our family. What happened to all the prayers offered on behalf of my family? How were they answered?

God gave me grace to get through those tumultuous years. Feeling overwhelmed, I would cry out to God, "What do I do with this? How can I cope?" After pouring out my heart, I would feel a peace settle upon my spirit. It was as though an invisible hand had lifted me. Often a Scripture I was reading would be exactly right for me. (I have many highlighted, dated verses that nourished me.) Sometimes a friend would call and offer me respite. In so many different ways, God let me know that He cared about me and my family. Yes, I sometimes wonder, why didn't God heal my husband too? But then I remind myself, God has written a different life script for me. He used just as much love and care to write my script as He did when He wrote Sandy's script.

One faithful God—two different kinds of prayer answers. In Hebrews chapter 11 verses 33-39, we read about these two responses to faithful prayers:

GROUP A:
[Some persons] *through faith conquered kingdoms, administered justice, and gained what was promised; who shut the mouths of lions, quenched the fury of the flames, and escaped the edge of the sword; whose weak-*

ness was turned to strength; and who became powerful in battle and routed foreign armies. Women received back their dead, raised to life again.

Some faced jeers and flogging, while still others were chained and put in prison. They were stoned; they were sawed in two; they were put to death by the sword. They went about in sheepskins and goatskins, destitute, persecuted and mistreated...These were all commended for their faith, yet none of them received what had been promised.

In answer to fervent prayers, Group A received deliverance now while Group B received endurance and grace to wait for its deliverance in heaven. Both groups exercised believing prayer that honoured God. Both groups were commended for their faith.

What are we to learn from this?

Prayer is about relationship more than about answers. Our earnest prayers do not convince a reluctant God to act on our behalf, but rather they provide an opportunity for us to open ourselves to God and to get to know Him. As we pour out our hearts and tell Him our hurts, we find that He listens. In reading the Bible, we receive His comfort and guidance. In our weakness, we learn to depend upon Him. Prayer is God's answer to our poverty, not a power we exercise to obtain an answer. The ..ght function of faith, in prayer and in life, is to open us up to God and to deliver us over to God.

I'm reminded of a small boy who ran to his father with a broken toy. "Fix this for me, Dad," he demanded. He was still of the age when a boy has absolute confidence that his father can fix anything. And being of an impatient nature, he wanted it fixed *now*.

One day, this wise father said, "Stay awhile, son, and watch me. Let's fix this together." Day after day, as they were working on the broken toy, heads together, talking softly, father and son got to know each other better. As the boy fetched screws and nails for his father and held certain parts while his father hammered and glued, he learned some important skills for his life's work.

God is like that father. He desires for us to bring our broken dreams, broken relationships, and broken bodies to Him. Often He does not fix them for us *now* but invites us to spend time with Him in a loving relationship, and in so doing we experience the comfort of His healing presence. And in the process, we learn that our prayers are answered— not when we are given what we asked for but when we are challenged to be what we can be.

In life, we need both kinds of prayer answers: the overt miraculous and the inside-ourselves miraculous. Both display the power and goodness of God. Both strengthen faith and bring glory to God.

When God heals now, give Him praise; when God does not heal now, give Him praise. No matter what the answer, know that God has acted in love and wisdom toward you. And in eternity, all will be healed.

God Is Good All the Time⁸⁶

It was dark and rainy when the buses, carrying teens fresh from the '95 Youth Weekend in Banff, Alberta, Canada, stopped for supper. Hours earlier, the youth leader had shouted from the podium, "God is good!"

"All the time!" the exuberant young people roared back.

After supper, a group of teens walked back to the bus. They saw the headlights of an oncoming car but thought it was far away. Seconds later, the car crashed into the middle of the group. Brakes squealed. Screams split the air. Three bodies thudded to the ground. Amanda Derksen, a grade eleven student from Waldheim, Saskatchewan, was instantly killed. Two other girls sustained injuries from which they recovered.

Young people from many churches came to Amanda's memorial service. They stood in huddles of silent grief. Subdued weeping punctuated the songs, the eulogy, and the sermon. Then the youth pastor rose and slowly walked toward the podium. A few short days ago, in a very different setting, he had led a group of eager youths in an enthusiastic chant: "God is good! God is good! God is good!" Tragedy had struck, but had God changed? Was He still good in this setting?

The pastor's eyes blurred as he looked across his audience of sombre faces. Taking a deep breath, he said, "God is good." Something happened in the audience: a stir of people shifting in their seats, tear-stained faces looking up expectantly. "God is good," the youth pastor repeated, his voice gaining strength.

"All the time," the teens mumbled through their tears.

How do we know that God is good when our lives feel bad? When circumstances threaten to crush us and prayers remain unanswered, where is God? Is He lovingly involved in our lives even then?

Could it be that our measure of God's goodness is wrong?

I believe it is. We've been conditioned to think of God as a doting parent whose function is to shield us from unpleasant circumstances. We have learned to equate the goodness of God with the "rightness" of our circumstances. We are like the little girl who, when she got what she wanted, exclaimed, "God must really like me!" Or conversely, when things weren't going her way, she pouted, "Why is God punishing me like this?"

King David did not make this mistake. He knew that God's goodness is based on His character traits of mercy and love, qualities that never change. David knew about adversities. Maligned by friends and family, hunted by King Saul, hiding in caves and fearing for his life, David poured out his anguish to God. Then he made an astonishing declaration: "Remember, O LORD, your great mercy and love, for they are from of old...according to your love remember me, for you are good, O LORD. Good and upright is the LORD."[87] In fact, David proclaimed the goodness of God in the many psalms he wrote.

"Give thanks to the LORD, for he is good; his love endures forever."[88]

"You are good, and what you do is good."[89]

"The LORD is good to all; he has compassion on all he has made."[90]

Our circumstances are not an accurate reflection of God's goodness. Whether life is good or bad, God's goodness, rooted in His character, is always the same. Knowing this, David could sing of the goodness of God, whether he was peacefully tending his father's sheep, or fearfully running from his enemies. "All the ways of the LORD are loving and faithful,"[91] he concludes. "Taste and see that the LORD is good; blessed is the man who takes refuge in him."[92] Therefore, God's goodness is the same on bad days as it is on good days.

People who attest to God's goodness in their lives do not experience an absence of trouble but rather have a keen awareness of God's presence in every situation. Some of my patients at a senior care home have shown me how this works in daily life.

While taking around morning medications, I would find an elderly couple enjoying their early morning coffee. The small woman had risen early to perk coffee exactly the way her husband liked it. Then, in grand style, she had poured it into Royal Albert china cups. As I entered, her husband, a tall gentleman with regal bearing, would greet me. We would chat a bit, and often he would end his conversation with the words, "God is good."

One day he told me a story I shall never forget. "We lived in Siberia during the Russian Revolution," he said. "One cold winter night, gypsies entered our home. We gave them food and lodging. The following day they left.

"We did our best to scour our home, but it was too late. The gypsies had brought smallpox into our home. One of our children became ill and died. Because the ground was frozen several metres deep, we buried our little son in a snowbank. We would give him a proper burial in the spring. A second son died also, followed by the death of our beautiful daughter. In the spring, we dug three little graves side by side. It was a very sad time for us."

I stood transfixed. I could not imagine such sorrow. But this wasn't the end of their hardships. Over the next few years, they had buried two more children. Moreover, under the Communist regime, life had become unbearable for this family. Seeking religious freedom, they left their home with just a few belongings and travelled to Moscow. Eventually they had been able to immigrate to Canada and start a new life. "We were among the lucky ones who got out," he said. "God has been good to us."

They had buried five children. They had lost their home, and country and almost all their possessions. In a foreign country, they endured endless struggles to get ahead. Yet I detected no bitterness or rancor—just a deep conviction that God is good, even when life is not.

Faith in God's goodness is not destroyed by hardships. On the contrary, life's storms create an opportunity to grow deeper into God's character. When we do, we will discover, to our glad surprise, that God is good all the time.

References

1 Numbers 14:9 NLT.

2 Numbers 13:30 ESV.

3 Joshua 14:12 NIV.

4 "The Landlady's Christmas Gift," printed in *Catholic Digest,* December 1991, PO Box 64090, St. Paul, MN 55164.

5 "Celebrate the Light," printed in the *Mennonite Brethren Herald,* December 9, 1994, 3-169 Riverton Ave., Winnipeg, MB, Canada R2L 2E5.

6 "Why Be Afraid?" printed in the *Mennonite Brethren Herald*, September 15, 1995.

7 Psalm 34:7.

8 "Gems of Truth: Pass It On," Reprinted with permission from *Daily Guideposts,* 1999, by Guideposts, Carmel, NY 10512.

9 Proverbs 11:25.

10 Hebrews 13:5; See also, Deuteronomy 31:6; Joshua 1:5.

11 John 15:16.

12 Ephesians 1:4-5.

13 "The Award Ceremony," printed in *With Magazine,* March/April 2002, under the title "The Jesus Cheer," Box 347, 722 Main St., Newton, KS 67114.

14 John 10:27,28.

15 2 Corinthians 4:6-7 CEV.

16 Philippians 4:13.

[17] 2 Corinthians 5:17-18.

[18] Ardis Whitman, *Woman's Day*, June 10, 1980.

[19] Anne Dueck, "Leaning Into The Curves," reprinted with permission from *Guideposts Magazine*, September 1990, Carmel, NY 10512.

[20] Psalm 16:11.

[21] Tim Hudson from cs-html-weekday-reply@PostOffice. Daily Inbox.com.

[22] "My Husband Has AIDS," printed in *Virtue* Magazine, May/June 1990.

[23] "When Life Is Unfair," printed in *Decision Magazine*, March 1991, 1300 Harmon Place, PO Box 779, Minneapolis, MN 55440-0779.

[24] See Genesis 3:1-5.

[25] See 2 Corinthians 10:12.

[26] Hebrews 1:3.

[27] See Romans 8:35-39.

[28] "Making Memories," printed in *Home Life Magazine*.

[29] Oswald Chambers, *Devotions for Morning and Evening*, 1994, page 435, Inspirational Press, 386 Park Avenue South, New York, NY 10016.

[30] "I Needed to Listen," printed in *Christian Woman*, November 10, 1999, PO Box 650, Punchbowl, NSW 2196, Australia.

[31] Zephaniah 3:17.

[32] "Jonathan's Passport," reprinted with permission from *Guideposts Magazine*, 1991.

[33] "Tattooed Angel," printed in the *Mennonite Brethren Herald*, December 20, 1991.

[34] "Lisa's Chicken," printed in *Alliance Life Magazine*, October 25, 1989.

[35] Philippians 4:19.

[36] "Watch Over My Son," printed in the *Mennonite Brethren Herald*, June 8, 2001.

37 "Esther's Rose," reprinted with permission from *Daily Guideposts*, 2004.

38 "She's Leaving Home," reprinted with permission from *Reader's Digest* (1100 Rene Levesque Blvd W, Montreal, Quebec, H3B 5H5) January 2001.

39 Ecclesiastes 12:11, AMP.

40 1 John 3:5.

41 "Poplar Trees and Children," reprinted with permission from *Daily Guideposts*, 2001.

42 Isaiah 54:13.

43 Jeremiah 24:6,7.

44 Isaiah 44:4.

45 Jeremiah 17:7,8 NRSV.

46 Psalm 145:8,9.

47 "The Light of His Presence," printed in *the Mennonite Brethren Herald*, November 10, 1995.

48 Isaiah 42:16.

49 "Lend Me Your Hope," printed in the *Mennonite Brethren Herald*, February 18, 1994.

50 "He's Holding Me," printed in *The Evangelical Baptist*, November/December 2003, 18 Louvigny, Lorraine, QC, Canada J6Z 1T7.

51 2 Samuel 22:17.

52 Isaiah 41:13.

53 Psalm 37:24.

54 Psalm 18:28.

55 "Facing Your Fear," printed in *With Magazine*, June 2000.

56 "No Room for Resentment," printed in *Christian Living*, May 1989, under the title "She found no need to be in anyone's will."

57 "More Life to Live," reprinted with permission from the *Reader's Digest*, November 2000.

58 Psalm 90:12.

59 "Singing in the Face of Death," printed in *The Canadian*

Nurse, November 1994, under the title "Hymns of Hope."

[60] Hebrews 10:35-36.

[61] Philippians 4:13.

[62] "What Love Built," reprinted with permission from Guideposts Magazine, November 2000.

[63] For more information on the work of Seeds of Hope, check out www.seedsofhopecm.com, e-mail seedsofhope@telus.net, or write PO Box 3474, Mission BC, V2V 4L1, Canada or Grace Brethren Church, 355 Panama Ave. Chico, CA 95973.

[64] "Gospel from the Grave," printed in *Mature Living*, February 2005, One LifeWay Plaza, Nashville, TN 37234-0175.

[65] For more information check out www.biblesforthepoor.org, e-mail biblesforthepoor@shaw.ca, or write to Bibles for the Poor Society, Box 593, Aldergrove B.C., Canada V4W 2V1, or P.O. Box 948 Sumas, Wash. 98295.

[66] Armin Schowalter, "Finally Free!" printed in *Decision Magazine*, October 1997.

[67] Susan Houle, "Snow White," printed in *The Center Magazine*, Spring 2002, Box 1350, Stafford, VA 22555.

[68] Isaiah 1:18.

[69] Tracy Anderson, "My Life Is Ruined," printed in *Campus Life Magazine*, November/December 2000, 465 Gundersen Dr., Carol Stream, IL 60188.

[70] Cathy Lescheid, "It's Not Fair!" printed in *Campus Life Magazine*, November/December 1999.

[71] Justin Manzey, "The Power of Forgiveness," printed in *With Magazine*, May/June 2001.

[72] Romans 5:8.

[73] "When Love Bridges the Gap," reprinted with permission from *Daily Guideposts*, 2003.

[74] Ingrid Trobisch, *Keeper Of The Springs*, Multnomah Publishers, Sisters, OR, 1997, page 56. I've added "and son" in parentheses.

[75] "Put Your Guilt to Rest," printed in *Light and Life*

Magazine, July/August 2002, PO Box 535002 Indianapolis, IN 46253-5002.

[76] See Philippians 3:13.

[77] 1 John 1:9, NLT.

[78] Philippians 3:14, NLT.

[79] Oswald Chambers, *Devotions for Morning and Evening,* 1994, page 25, Inspirational Press, 386 Park Avenue South, New York, NY 10016.

[80] Cathy Lescheid, "Why Can't I Believe?" printed in *With Magazine,* March 2000.

[81] "Mark's Miracle" took place in December 1993 and January 1994.

[82] "When You No Longer Hear the Music," printed in *War Cry Magazine,* November 24, 2001, 615 Slaters Lane, PO Box 269, Alexandria, VA 22314.

[83] Fred Shannon, "Abundant Grace," printed in *Shantymen Magazine,* November 2003, 1885 Clements Road, Unit 226, Pickering, ON, Canada L1W 3V4.

[84] Colossians 1:27.

[85] "One Faithful God—Two Prayer Answers," printed in *Church of God Evangel Magazine,* September 2004, 1080 Montgomery Ave., Cleveland, TN 37320-2250.

[86] "God Is Good All the Time," printed in *War Cry Magazine,* August 17, 2002.

[87] Psalm 25:6-8.

[88] Psalm 107:1.

[89] Psalm 119:68.

[90] Psalm 145:9.

[91] Psalm 25:10.

[92] Psalm 34:8.